Gwendolyn Brooks

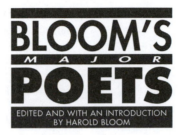

BLOOM'S MAJOR POETS

D0208524

CURRENTLY AVAILABLE

BLOOM'S MAJOR DRAMATISTS	BLOOM'S MAJOR NOVELISTS	BLOOM'S MAJOR POETS	BLOOM'S MAJOR SHORT STORY WRITERS
Aeschylus	Jane Austen	Maya Angelou	Jorge Luis Borges
Aristophanes	The Brontës	Elizabeth Bishop	Italo Calvino
Bertolt Brecht	Willa Cather	William Blake	Raymond Carver
Anton Chekhov	Stephen Crane	Gwendolyn Brooks	Anton Chekhov
Henrik Ibsen	Charles Dickens	Robert Browning	Joseph Conrad
Ben Johnson	William Faulkner	Geoffrey Chaucer	Stephen Crane
Christopher Marlowe	F. Scott Fitzgerald	Sameul Taylor Coleridge	William Faulkner
Arthur Miller	Nathaniel Hawthorne	Dante	F. Scott Fitzgerald
Eugene O'Neill	Ernest Hemingway	Emily Dickinson	Nathaniel Hawthorne
Shakespeare's Comedies	Henry James	John Donne	Ernest Hemingway
Shakespeare's Histories	James Joyce	H.D.	O. Henry
Shakespeare's Romances	D. H. Lawrence	T. S. Eliot	Shirley Jackson
Shakespeare's Tragedies	Toni Morrison	Robert Frost	Henry James
George Bernard Shaw	John Steinbeck	Seamus Heaney	James Joyce
Neil Simon	Stendhal	Homer	Franz Kafka
Oscar Wilde	Leo Tolstoy	Langston Hughes	D.H. Lawrence
Tennessee Williams	Mark Twain	John Keats	Jack London
August Wilson	Alice Walker	John Milton	Thomas Mann
	Edith Wharton	Sylvia Plath	Herman Melville
	Virginia Woolf	Edgar Allan Poe	Flannery O'Connor
		Poets of World War I	Edgar Allan Poe
		Shakespeare's Poems & Sonnets	Katherine Anne Porter
		Percy Shelley	J. D. Salinger
		Alfred, Lord Tennyson	John Steinbeck
		Walt Whitman	Mark Twain
		William Carlos Williams	John Updike
		William Wordsworth	Eudora Welty
		William Butler Yeats	

COMPREHENSIVE RESEARCH
AND STUDY GUIDE

Gwendolyn Brooks

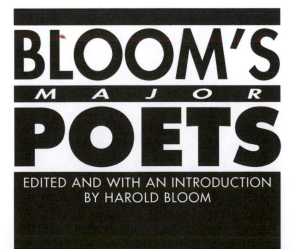

BLOOM'S *MAJOR* POETS

EDITED AND WITH AN INTRODUCTION
BY HAROLD BLOOM

Printed and bound in the United States of America.

First Printing
1 3 5 7 9 8 6 4 2

Library of Congress Cataloging-in-Publication Data
Gwendolyn Brooks / Harold Bloom, ed.
      p. cm. —(Bloom's major poets)
      Includes bibliographical references and index.
      ISBN 0-7910-6815-3
      1. Brooks, Gwendolyn, 1917—Criticism and interpretation. 2.
Women and literature–United States—History—20th century. 3.
African Americans in literature. I. Series.
      PS3503.R7244 Z66 2002
      811.54'—dc21   2002004480

Chelsea House Publishers
1974 Sproul Road, Suite 400
Broomall, PA 19008-0914

The Chelsea House World Wide Web address is http://www.chelseahouse.com

Contributing Editor: Robb Erskine

Layout by EJB Publishing Services

CONTENTS

USER'S GUIDE

This volume is designed to present biographical, critical, and bibliographical information on the author and the author's best-known or most important short stories. Following Harold Bloom's editor's note and introduction is a concise biography of the author that discusses major life events and important literary accomplishments. A plot summary of each story follows, tracing significant themes, patterns, and motifs in the work. An annotated list of characters supplies brief information on the main characters in each story. As with any study guide, it is recommended that the reader read the story beforehand, and have a copy of the story being discussed available for quick reference.

A selection of critical extracts, derived from previously published material, follows each character list. In most cases, these extracts represent the best analysis available from a number of leading critics. Because these extracts are derived from previously published material, they will include the original notations and references when available. Each extract is cited, and readers are encouraged to check the original publication as they continue their research. A bibliography of the author's writings, a list of additional books and articles on the author and their work, and an index of themes and ideas conclude the volume.

ABOUT THE EDITOR

Harold Bloom is Sterling Professor of the Humanities at Yale University and Henry W. and Albert A. Berg Professor of English at the New York University Graduate School. He is the author of over 20 books, and the editor of more than 30 anthologies of literary criticism.

Professor Bloom's works include *Shelly's Mythmaking* (1959), *The Visionary Company* (1961), *Blake's Apocalypse* (1963), *Yeats* (1970), *A Map of Misreading* (1975), *Kabbalah and Criticism* (1975), *Agon: Toward a Theory of Revisionism* (1982), *The American Religion* (1992), *The Western Canon* (1994), and *Omens of Millennium: The Gnosis of Angels, Dreams, and Resurrection* (1996). *The Anxiety of Influence* (1973) sets forth Professor Bloom's provocative theory of the literary relationships between the great writers and their predecessors. His most recent books include *Shakespeare: The Invention of the Human*, a 1998 National Book Award finalist, *How to Read and Why* (2000), and *Stories and Poems for Extremely Intelligent Children of All Ages* (2001).

Professor Bloom earned his Ph.D. from Yale University in 1955 and has served on the Yale faculty since then. He is a 1985 MacArthur Foundation Award recipient and served as the Charles Eliot Norton Professor of Poetry at Harvard University in 1987–88. In 1999 he was awarded the prestigious American Academy of Arts and Letters Gold Medal for Criticism. Professor Bloom is the editor of several other Chelsea House series in literary criticism, including BLOOM'S MAJOR SHORT STORY WRITERS, BLOOM'S MAJOR NOVELISTS, BLOOM'S MAJOR DRAMATISTS, MODERN CRITICAL INTERPRETATIONS, MODERN CRITICAL VIEWS, and BLOOM'S BIOCRITIQUES.

EDITOR'S NOTE

My Introduction centers upon the controlled pathos of "The Mother."

Kathryne V. Lindberg, commenting on "The Mother," commends Brooks for "at once humanizing and equivocating over victim and agent," while Maria K. Mootry notes the oblique effectiveness of "The Bean Eaters."

"We Real Cool" moves Gary Smith to contrast urban reality to romance in the poem, after which, D. H. Melhem analyzes Brooks's voice in "Bronzeville Women in a Red Hat."

"The Riot" is viewed by Charles L. James as marking a new mode in Brooks, while "Queen of the Blues" is illuminated by Gary Smith and George E. Kent, among others.

Harold Bloom

Gwendolyn Brooks (1917-2000) lived a long and distinguished life, marked by her continuous devotion to writing the poetry of her people. Her early poem, "The Mother," remains an impressive dramatic monologue, restrained alike in its pathos and its irony, and curiously wrought in emotional contraries:

> Abortions will not let you forget.
> You remember the children you got that you did not get,
> The damp small pulps with a little or with no hair,
> The singers and workers that never handled the air.
> You will never neglect or beat
> Them, or silence or buy with a sweet.
> You will never wind up the sucking-thumb
> Or scuttle off ghosts that come.
> You will never leave them, controlling your luscious sigh,
> Return for a snack of them, with gobbling mother-eye.

It is difficult to describe the effective balance of this chant. What precisely is the speaker's attitude towards her unborn children? Handling the air is very different for "singers and workers," and the imagery of "luscious," "snack," and "gobbling" turns upon an implicit critique of the speaker's narcissism, while still expressing her implicit loss.

It is the second verse-paragraph that achieves a more disturbing level of intensity, in which something like a lament rises (though very obliquely) for those never allowed to be:

> You were born, you had body, you died.
> It is just that you never giggled or planned or cried.

A dispassionate lament is an irony, and so is the poem's conclusion:

> Believe me, I loved you all.
> Believe me, I knew you, though faintly, and I loved, I loved
> you all.

Brooks later became a poet of social protest, joining in the principal currents of African-American poetry in the last third of the twentieth century. She became more direct, and doubtless a liberating force. The enigmas of her earlier poems, like "The Mother," to me seem imaginatively richer.

Gwendolyn Brooks

On June 7, 1917 Gwendolyn Brooks was the first of two children born to David Anderson Brooks and Keziah Corinne (Wims) Brooks. Born at her grandmother's house in Topeka, Kansas; approximately one month after her birth she was taken back to her parents' home in Chicago where she lived for the rest of her life.

Gwendolyn's passion for writing and interest in poetry began at an early age and by the age of thirteen she published her first poem in the magazine *American Childhood*. During her years in high school, she met the poet James Weldon Johnson who encouraged her to read and emulate poets like T.S. Eliot and e.e. cummings. This chance meeting was inspirational for Brooks and by the age of sixteen she had published over seventy poems. Her notoriety was further fueled by her association with Langston Hughes who encouraged her to continue reading and writing and often wrote about Gwendolyn's promise and talent in his newspaper column.

In 1935 Brooks graduated from Englewood High School and went to Wilson Junior College to study English. After graduating in 1936, Brooks unsuccessfully tried to obtain a full-time writing position at the *Chicago Defender*, where she had been a weekly contributor to the column "Lights and Shadows," but she was turned away. She worked as a maid in a few homes and then later as a secretary in several offices before she got a job working as a publicity director for the Chicago chapter of the National Association for the Advancement of Colored People (NAACP) youth council.

On September 17, 1939 she married Henry Blakely and over the next few years they both began attending Inez Cunningham Starks' poetry workshops where Starks furthered Brooks's knowledge of contemporary poets and introduced Brooks to the bubbling poetic scene in Chicago. The workshop discussions were open and honest and at times a bit brutal. During this time Starks and others critiqued Brooks's work thoroughly. Brooks grew from this experience and in 1943 she won a poetry award from the Midwestern Writer's Conference. Two years later her first collection of poetry *A Street in Bronzeville* (1945) was published through Harper & Row.

This first collection mirrored her own experiences in the suburb of Chicago called Bronzeville. The collection is broken into two distinct sections with the first detailing the average, day-to-day occurrences of people Brooks knew in Bronzeville. The poetry is marked by Brooks's combination of its simple language and direct sentences with a strict adherence to poetic metre and structure including a few sonnets. The second part of the collection details the unfair treatment of African Americans in the military during WWII. The collection was met with praise and shortly after it was published she was awarded a Guggenheim fellowship. This notoriety was furthered when she became the first African American to win the Pulitzer Prize for her second collection, *Annie Allen* (1949).

In 1953 Brooks demonstrated her versatility with the novel *Maud Martha*. This autobiographical novel explored the racist, sexist, and other oppressive forces surrounding an African American woman before, during, and after WWII. Her fourth publication, *The Bean Eaters* (1960), reflected Brooks's growing interest in civil rights issues and marks the beginning of her experimentation with free verse. During the period between publications Brooks taught creative writing at several universities, including Columbia College (Chicago), Northeastern Illinois University, Elmhurst College, Columbia University, Clay College of New York, and the University of Wisconsin.

Her poetic style and interest in Black Studies was forever changed after attending the Second Black Writers' Conference at Fisk University. At this conference she met Amiri Baraka (formerly LeRoi Jones), Ron Milner, and Haki R. Madhubuti (formerly Don L. Lee). Their work and conviction for civil rights and black cultural nationalism inspired her, and her next work *In the Mecca* (1968) reflected this spiritual change. Most of the poems in the collection deal with the events taking place in the tenement building in Chicago called Mecca. Her poems in this collection are vivid and powerful descriptions of poverty, social inequality, death, and spiritual loss. The collection also included poems about the murders of Medgar Evars and Malcolm X along with a few poems detailing the activities of a local gang: the Blackstone Rangers. Her attention to human emotions and reality were noted and she was appointed Poet Laureate of Illinois; a position that she held until her death.

Her poetic expression in *Riot* (1969) and *Family Pictures* (1970) was heavily influenced by the social and political turbulence of the late 1960's, and her poetry became more community oriented. Her autobiography *Report from Part One* (1972) illustrates her spiritual change during this time as well documenting the events leading up to the 1969 conference at Fisk University. The subtle optimistic hints of social equality from her earlier work were replaced by the disenchantment of the civil rights movements and black power movements. Her next works *Beckonings* (1975) and *To Disembark* (1981) reflect this frustration and many of the poems promote anarchy and violence as a way to achieve social equality.

She continued to write poetry and became more involved in bringing poetry to the people through public readings, workshops, classes, and contests. In 1983 she published *Very Young Poets,* and in 1990 she became the first American to receive the Society of Literature Award from the University of Thessalonika, Athens, Greece. Her later books include *Children Coming Home (1991)* and the second half of her autobiography *Report from Part Two* (1995). Her involvement in community organizations and her more than fifty honorary degrees demonstrate the impact her poetry has had on the American society. She received the lifetime achievement award from the National Endowment for the Arts, the National Book Foundation Award for Distinguished Contribution to American Letters, induction into the National Women's Hall of Fame, and in 1994 the National Endowment for the Arts awarded her the governments highest honor for achievement in the humanities: the Jefferson Lecturer.

In a powerful demonstration of her impact on the world, on June 7, 1997 over eighty poets and writers gather at the Harold Washington Library and held a special five-hour reading of Brooks's poetry. On December 3, 2000, four years after the death of her husband Henry Blakely, Jr., Gwendolyn Brooks died at the age of 83. She had been suffering from cancer for some time and she died peacefully in her bed with family and friends reading to her.

CRITICAL ANALYSIS OF

"The Mother"

As a poet, one of Gwendolyn Brooks's best talents is her precise use of grammar and vocabulary. Her word choice, sentence structure and use of punctuation are all used in coordination with one another to express her topic, tone, and emotion in the poem. In the poem "The Mother" (1945) originally published in Brooks's first collection of poetry *A Street in Bronzeville*, she addresses the controversial issue of abortion, but she does not simply take a side; she demonstrates the anguish and remorse the mother has for her unborn child, yet Brooks does not portray the mother expressing regret. Her ability to simultaneously address both pro choice and pro-life views encourages the audience to appreciate the issue from both sides.

The opening theme of "The Mother" centers around an aborted child or children and a remorseful mother remembering the child. She personifies the noun abortion demonstrating that the procedure—an abortion— is not just a quick outpatient operation but something that becomes part of the mother forever. Brooks confirms that the abortion is representative of a life, a gift the "you got that you did not get." The description of the aborted fetus as "damp small pulps with little or no hair" in line three depicts an awkward moment when a mother may see the aborted fetus after the procedure. In the next eight lines, Brooks describes the mother thinking about all the things she will not be able to do with the child. She keeps this description realistic describing both the good and the bad things that the mother will never experience with a child. The realism in this section is important because it identifies some of the things that may have persuaded the mother to get an abortion.

Brooks elaborates on some of the things parents have to do for their children like discouraging them from sucking their thumb or scaring away ghosts and contrasts this with the subtle, pleasant parental moment of turning and stealing a final glimpse of a child, "controlling your luscious sigh" and symbolically gobbling them up with a maternal glance. But these are only hypothetical thoughts of what could have been, for the next stanza thrusts the audience into the mother's reality.

The mother is alone and speaking now in the first person. Her time is spent listening to the voices of her aborted children in the wind. The voices trigger the physical pains of a contraction and the mother symbolically suckles the "dim dears" to her breasts. The mother, addressing the children as "Sweets," apologizes for her actions. She is not confident that she does in fact have anything for which to apologize. In these lines, Brooks uses the subordinate conjunction "if" to demonstrate that the mother is not sure if she has sinned if she has stolen life from the child. She does not know if she had that power or if the child even knew they had life. What she does know is that she will always remember them, and she wants them to know that "...even in my deliberateness I was not deliberate."

In the next line the mother reveals that she does not want to come across as whining about her actions or coming up with any excuses. She does not want to go back and change the past. She is unsure if the child ever had life stating:

> You were never made
> But that too, I am afraid,
> Is faulty: oh, what shall I say, how is the truth to be said?

She does not know what the truth is. She does not pass judgment on herself for the decision that she made or condemn herself for her action, nor does she try to blame anyone else. She reverts to the only "facts" she has. "You were born, You had body, You died." She does not know if there was any consciousness or understanding, just as she does not know if the aborted children can hear her at all.

The poem ends with her direct expression of her love for them all.

> Believe me, I loved you all
> Believe me, I knew you, though faintly, and I loved, I loved you
> All.

She does not know if what she did was right or wrong. She simply wants to acknowledge that it happened, and she is responsible.

Brooks does not describe the mother as regretting her decision. She describes a woman who made a decision based on whatever circumstances surrounded her life. She was able to make this decision.

"The Mother"

BEVERLY GUY-SHEFTALL ON A "BRONZEVILLE" MOTHER

[Beverly Guy-Sheftall is the director of the Women's Research and Resource Center and assistant professor of English at Spelman College. She is the co-editor of Sturdy Black Bridges: Visions of Black Women in Literature and co-editor of Sage: A Scholarly Journal on Black Women. In this extract, Guy-Sheftall discusses the why this woman may have decided to have an abortion]

Brooks also explores the impact of poverty on the lives of her women characters; "the mother" deals with a poor woman who has had a number of abortions, and who experiences anxiety and anguish as a result of these decisions. In the appendix of her autobiography, Brooks refers to her as "hardly your crowned and praised and 'customary' Mother; but a Mother not unfamiliar, who decides that *she* rather than her World, will kill her children" (*Report*, 184). Accepting full responsibility for her "crime," she nevertheless remains ambivalent about her actions and exactly what she has done. Although she realizes that she has shielded her unborn babies from the harsh realities of the life they were sure to lead, she also admits having stolen from them whatever joys they might have been able to experience. She wonders if she had that right.

> ... if I sinned, if I seized
> Your luck
> And your lives from your unfinished reach,
> If I stole your births and your names,
> Your straight baby tears and your games,
> Your stilted or lovely loves, your tumults, your marriages,
>   aches, and your deaths,
> If I poisoned the beginnings of your breaths,
> Believe that even in my deliberateness I was not deliberate.
>   (*WGB*, 51)

Throughout the poem, one has the feeling that if circumstances had been different, if she had been able to provide adequately for them, they would have been allowed to live. Ironically, it was her deep concern for them as well as her own situation, which caused her to have the abortions.

> Believe me, I loved you all.
> Believe me, I knew you, though faintly, and I loved you, I
>   loved you
> All.
>   (*WGB*, 6)

She knew perfectly well what their fate would have been.

> You will never neglect or beat
> Them, or silence or buy with a sweet,
> You will never wind up the sucking-thumb
> or scuttle off ghosts that come.
> You will never leave them, controlling your luscious
>   sigh,
> Return for a snack of them, with gobbling mother-eye.
>   (*WGB*, 5)

Although George Kent criticizes the poem for failing "to convey the attitude of the author toward her subject—the several abortions of the mother," there is no question in my mind nor probably in the minds of women who have had abortions for similar or even other reasons where Brooks's sympathies lie.

> —Beverly Guy-Sheftall, "The Women of Bronzeville." *A Life Distilled: Gwendolyn Brooks, Her Poetry and Fiction*. Ed. Maria K Mootry and Gary Smith (Urbana, IL: University of Illinois Press, 1987): pp. 156-157.

D. H. MELHEM ON EMOTIONS IN THE POEM

[D. H. Melhem is an accomplished novelist, dramatist, and critic. A few of her publications are *Blight* (1995), *Children of the House Afire* (1976), and *Heroism and the New Black Poetry (1990)*. She is currently the Vice President of the International Women's Writing Guild. In this selection, Melhem analyzes the complex emotions that the mother in this poem is experiencing.]

"[T]he mother" is a dramatic monologue on abortion, a controversial topic then, as now. She comments: "Hardly your crowned and praised and 'customary' Mother; but a Mother not unfamiliar, who decides that *she*, rather than her World, will kill her children. The decision is not nice, not simple, and the emotional consequences are neither nice nor simple" (*RPO*, 184).

The poet employs full rhyme with a touch of slant in this thirty-two-line poem, very irregularly metered. The first stanza rhymes five couplets; the second alternates rhyme in the first six lines, then continues the couplet pattern. The meter, rolling insistent, often anapestic, conveys the profound agitation of the speaker. Tonal control, especially in the first stanza, heightens tension. The mother begins rhetorically, "Abortions will not let you forget," addressing the reader/listener in impersonal second person. She reviews the loss judiciously: the children will not be neglected; she will not be burdened. But during the second stanza, her defenses fall away: "I have heard in the voices of the wind the voices of my dim killed children." The woman then justifies herself to the aborted children, confessing that her "crime" was not "deliberate." She wanted to shield them from a painful existence. She loved them all, she insists, the last line universal, emphatic: "All."

—D. H. Melhem, "A Street in Bronzeville." *Gwendolyn Brooks: Poetry and the Heroic Voice.* (Lexington, Kentucky: The University Press of Kentucky, 1987): pp. 23-24.

TOKS PEARSE ON A MOTHER'S RESPONSIBILITY

[Toks Pearse is a well-known and respected Nigerian essayist and literary critic who coordinates the University without Walls program at Chicago State University. In this extract Pearse analyzes the emotional impact of an abortion on the woman in the poem.]

At the core of this poem is the notion of the responsibility of womanhood. It is a monologue and a lament of one woman which ultimately transcends the worries of one person and becomes the agony of a community, even of humanity.

A murder has been committed, a child is killed, human blood has been spilled and leaves a trail of guilt "abortions will not let you forget." Human life has been deprived of life, deprived of a future, even of a real presence.

Murder is bad enough, but what manner of woman would poison the umbilical cord of her own children? This woman's lament is heart-rending. Her admission of guilt is evidence of her extreme pain. "I have heard in the voices of the wind the voices of my dim killed children"—"If I poisoned the beginnings of your breaths, Believe that even in my deliberateness I was not deliberate." Now she has no children to play with, no one with whom to reciprocate love, care, tears of joy and tears of sorrow—all the experience of wanting and being wanted—an enriched experience of being.

Gwendolyn Brooks is a poet of the people hence explication of her poems must be sought from race-communal perspectives. "The Mother" is about individual pain, but the poem also strikes a chord on the matriarchy of African antiquity. As the Sotho of South Africa say, "touch the women and you strike the rock of the land." In the same spirit of maternal potency, the Yoruba people of Nigeria assert, "Iyani wura, omo lowo"—"Mother is gold, and children, the currency wrought from its ore." African societies view maternity as a blessing from the gods. In support of that belief, African literature is replete with the notion that barrenness is a woman's payback for evil sorcery. (. . .)

For a people plagued by the fear of communal disintegration, and for a people who live in a communal environment where manual family labor is key to economic survival, children are precious and motherhood revered. This is the cultural backcloth from which Gwendolyn Brooks fashions her poem. So in reading this poem, we are compelled to ask ourselves: What manner of woman would destroy her own life-line, stop the flow of life in its tracks and commit such a dastardly crime against nature? What type of woman is "The Mother" who will not mother her children, but would rather murder them. The genius of Gwendolyn Brooks is her ability to let the reader see that "The Mother," a self-confessed fetus killer is not a common criminal, but a sensitive woman overwhelmed by the politics of experience.

—Toks Pearse, "On Gwendolyn's Poem, 'The Mother.'" In *Say That the River Turns: The Impact of Gwendolyn Brooks*, ed. Haki R. Madhubuti (Chicago: Third World Press, 1987): pp. 76-78.

KATHRYNE V. LINDBERG ON ABORTION IN THE POEM

[Kathryne V. Lindberg is a scholar and writer who has been published in *Paideuma: A Journal Devoted to Ezra Pound, Discourse Journal for Theoretical Studies in Media and Culture, Boundary 2: An International Journal of Literature and Culture, Massachusetts Review: A Quarterly of Literature the Arts and Public Affair, and Talisman: A Journal of Contemporary Poetry and Poetics*. In this extract Lindberg discusses Brooks' ability to show the emotional complexity of having an abortion.]

Brooks's 1967 announcement of a different public role for herself as poet, along with her embrace of the evolving role of New Black, might have been impossible and surely would not have been very forceful if she had not threaded a consistent meditation on racial and artistic self-construction—and reconstructions of racial and sexual otherness—through her work.

Brooks has always addressed and continues to address difficult issues, including those often decorously silent intimate traumas of abortion, color caste, domestic abuse, alienation, and motherhood in poverty. Defiant in the face of a painful history of racist lies and false consciousness that refuses to yield a "useable past," she has actively fashioned models of personal and communal dignity as poetic blueprints for cultural survival. An early poem like "the mother" (*A Street in Bronzeville*, 1945) adumbrates her later focus on rejected, imperiled, and criminalized urban youth, even as it admits of wildly different ethos and messages: from an anti-abortion plea to a manifesto of women's choice and self-determination. This poem in particular continues to garner classroom and critical response for its complex deconstructions of subjectivity and/or the androcentric lyric tradition. As Barbara Johnson has noted, Brooks bends the genre of apostrophe by addressing the literally doubly victimized, the imaginatively doubly redeemed, and inextricably compounds nonmother and unborn as agent and object of abortion.

Brooks manages to convey the force of desire, regret and affirmation without sentimentalizing the role of mother or erasing the horrors of unrealized pasts and futures:

> ABORTIONS will not let you forget.
> You remember the children you got that you did not get,
> The damp small pulps with a little or with no hair,
> The singers and workers that never handled the air.
> You will never neglect or beat
> Them, or silence or buy with a sweet.
>   (*WGB*, 5)

After that first stanza, which complicates the ontological and epistemological categories generically fixed by personal lyric and the address of apostrophe, the subject—and here both positions of aborted relationships share objecthood and agency—switches from the general or colloquial "you" to an only more apparently fixed "I" that promises but fails to represent a single point of view or viable position, if only because it is addressed both to the unborn and the unknowing audience. Characteristically, Brooks both invites and inhibits identification as well as easy judgment from above and outside:

> Believe that even in my deliberateness I was not deliberate.
> Though why should I whine,
> Whine that the crime was other than mine?
> Since anyhow you are dead.
> Or rather, or instead,
> You were never made.
>   (*WGB*, 5–6)

If Brooks there achieves in an exemplary fashion the virtually impossible task of at once humanizing and equivocating over victim and agent—of making present, speaking as and to, those who definitively never were—she elsewhere works a similarly undecidable agency into the public arena of city streets and community. In fundamental ways, she has come increasingly to violate fixed definitions of gender and race roles as well as systems of representation and cultural reproduction.

> —Kathryne V. Lindberg, "Whose Canon? Gwendolyn Brooks: Founder at the Center of the 'Margins.'" *Gendered Modernisms: American Women Poets and Their Readers*, eds. Margaret Dickie and Thomas Travisano (University of Pennsylvania Press, 1996).

B. J. Bolden on A Mother's Memory

[B. J. Bolden is a literary critic and a professor at Chicago State University in the Department of English, Speech, and Modern Languages. She is also the director of the Gwendolyn Brooks Center for Black Literature and Creative Writing. Her current research project is documenting the Chicago Renaissance literacy movement between 1935 and 1950. In this excerpt Bolden discusses how the memory of the abortion is traumatic for the woman in the poem.]

One of Brooks' most memorable character vignettes is a poignant portrayal of a mother who understands the responsibilities of her life and meets them head on, even in the face of her own grief. In "the mother," Brooks creates a dramatic monologue to permit the ghetto mother of an aborted child to tell her own story of loss. It is amazingly ironic that the poem is still deemed one of Brooks' most powerful poems given the searing social statement it makes about a topic which, historically, has caused major dissension in America. But Brooks' speaker endears herself to the reader by assuming full responsibility for her act and sharing the inner trauma that will be her very own infinite pain.

The speaker opens the poem in an inchoate second-person voice as she haltingly broaches a topic that in the 1940s seldom found a receptive audience:

> Abortions will not let you forget.
> You remember the children you got that you did not
> > get,
> The damp small pulps with a little or with no hair. (21)

Once the mother finds her own sorrowful voice and lingers over a haunting description of her lost children, she acknowledges, in a forlorn tone, that she can never "Return for a snack of them, with gobbling mother-eye." The emotional momentum of the telling is a psychological breakthrough for the anguished mother, who finds the strength, in the second verse, to take ownership of her deed and her pain. She reveals: "I have heard in the voices of the wind the voices of my dim killed children." The vague "you" of the opening stanza is now "I" as the mother moves from telling the sense of absence that will torment another to claiming the pain of maternal absence as her own. She embraces her body as the intended vessel for the aborted child in lines that may stunningly be likened to the act of childbirth:

> I have contracted. I have eased
> My dim dears at the breasts they could never suck. (21)

And once the flood-gate opens, mother-memories gush through as she considers that if she has "sinned," her "crime" was not as intentional as it was necessary; she states: "Believe that even in my deliberateness I was not deliberate." And, finally, the mother makes an impassioned plea to her unborn children to believe that in spite of her deed, she did love them:

> Believe me, I loved you all.
> Believe me, I knew you, though faintly, and I loved, I
>   loved you
> All. (22)

The haunting refrains of a ghetto mother whose own struggle to survive will not permit her to support a new life is supported by the formal structure of the poem. The shifting metrical pattern of the poem parallels the junctures where the mother struggles, thoughtfully, to examine her own feelings about the abortion. The sudden reversal from iambic to anapestic meter in the repetition of "You will never," "I have heard," "I have contracted," and "I have said" illuminate the magnitude of the mother's loss. The use of rhymed couplets to convey information about the aborted child signals the memories associated with childlike melodies while the lines that point to the child's death are more somber and devoid of rhyme.

In a differing angle of the racial trials of the Black community, viewed from a gender perspective, Brooks makes a social commentary on the pain caused by both intraracial and interracial color hierarchies.

—B. J. Bolden, "A Street in Bronzeville (1945): A Blueprint of America's *Urban Landscape.*" *Urban Rage in Bronzeville: Social Commentary in the Poetry of Gwendolyn Brooks*, 1945-1960, (Chicago: Third World Press, 1999): pp. 26-28.

CRITICAL ANALYSIS OF
"The Bean Eaters"

This poem is the title poem of Brooks's fourth publication *The Bean Eaters* (1960), and it marks the beginning of Brooks's departure from her non-political poetry. Many of the poems in this collection deal with topics of a more politically aware nature and her tone about racism, suffering, and death escalate throughout this collection. In particular the title poem "The Bean Eaters" reveals Brooks's outlook on an elderly couple whose dietary habits reveal a great deal about their lives.

The major theme throughout this poem is that of the ordinary progression of time as a couple grows closer to death. Whether this death is spiritual or physical or both, Brooks keeps the events simple and the language is direct with only a few words having more than two syllables. The use of such basic language adds to the image of the couple's simple life together.

As is the case in much of Brooks's poetry, her word usage and punctuation play a large role in the interpretation and rhythm of the poem. The fact that the poem begins with the direct statement of the dietary habits of the old couple is exemplary of their desperation. The first theme introduced in the poem, the couple's eating habit, sets the tone for what follows—a tone that is not one of comfort or leisure but survival. Brooks chooses to begin the poem discussing not what they do for a living or how large their family is or even how long they have been married, but how they survive by eating beans. Because the focus seems to be on subsistence, Brooks does not reveal much about their relationship with one another. The reader can only guess as to whether the elderly couple is happy or in love. The second line of the poem further establishes the meager situation describing the couple as an "old yellow pair" going through a daily routine while they wait for death.

The use of the word pair here is striking as it indicates little more than existence. It is not a term usually associated with people in love, nor does it suggest anything animate. Furthermore, they are a yellow pair. While the use of the color yellow could be a suggestion of the pair's friendship, it seems to work as an additional adjective further explaining how old they are. In the same way that paper will begin to change color when it ages, the old pair age and become yellow and brittle. Brooks's attention to the meaning of color should not go unnoticed and the possible use of the color yellow to represent an illness such as jaundice is likely. Another possible explanation for the couple looking a bit yellow in color, if combined with the description of tobacco crumbs in the last line of the poem, brings to mind the discoloration associated with the stains from smoking cigarettes—yellow stains on the walls, clothes, furniture, and fingers.

The second line continues the recurring image of food describing the couple engaging in their nightly dinner routine. Brooks sets up the routine as being commonplace using the oxymoron "casual affair" to simultaneously reinforce their basic need for food while also suggesting that the pair try to make the event more regal. This juxtaposition continues in the next line with the description of the dinnerware being plain chipware. Chipware, an obvious description of damaged dinnerware, is by itself an oxymoron, but it is further downplayed by the adjective plain. Moreover, they are not eating on a table rather "plain and creaking wood." The table setting is completed with "tin flatware." Brooks's attention to such quality is a demonstration of the unimportance of fancy things. Her use of the oxymorons allow the reader to see that the manner in which they survive is not the issue. The fact that they have managed to survive is what is important.

While there is not a set rhythm in the first stanza, a melody is established. A slow steady progression leads in to the next stanza where we learn that the pair is "Mostly Good." Brooks chooses not to overemphasize their good nature using the word mostly to downplay their benevolence while also returning to the "mostly" used in the first stanza. It is also important to notice the use of capital letters for both mostly and good. Often in literature the capitalization of a word suggests a reference to religion, often to God. If this is the case, the capitalization suggests that it is a statement about the type of good meant by Brooks. This pair is religious and looks to some dogma as a basis for right and wrong, but just as with the other aspects of their life, they do not excel in their religious duties, but merely subsist.

In the next line Brooks reminds us of the mortality of the pair stating that they "…have lived their day," suggesting that the two will not experience anything new. Although they are in the twilight of their lives, the two do not complain; they follow the pattern that they have established. They put on their clothes and keep things tidy out of habit.

In the final stanza, Brooks uses an ellipsis (…) to demonstrate either the exclusion of certain memories or the passage of time as they remember their lives. Even in this reminiscence, Brooks maintains the realistic outlook of the couple as they remember, "with twinkles and twinges," covering both the positive and negative moments. All aspects of their lives are remembered as the poem returns to the opening mealtime image. Brooks takes great care to add just a bit more of a dramatic touch to the final description of the meal by including that "…this old yellow pair…have lived their day" in a rented back room cluttered with the odds and ends of no material value but that have the sentimental value that is required for a pair who have lived a life of subsistence: "beads, receipts, dolls, and cloths,/tobacco crumbs, vases and fringes."

"The Bean Eaters"

D. H. MELHEM ON AGING IN *THE BEAN EATERS*

[In this extract, Melhem provides a brief description of the treatment of aging in the poem "The Bean Eaters" as well as several other poems from the collection *The Bean Eaters* (1960).]

These poems, scattered throughout the volume, cluster around four main subjects: aging, romance, philosophy, and children, with single poems on fame, nature, and faith, the last also treated in several pieces above.

The title poem, "The Bean Eaters," irregularly metered and rhymed, describes an "old yellow pair" who are "Mostly Good." They continue the routines of their lives, strong in mutual affection and shared memories. Because they are indigent, their conventional lives have neither troubled nor impressed the world. In subdued tone, they echo the endurance of Mrs. Small. Their reward for a "good" life is an old age of poverty, symbolized by the beans they can afford. Their fate implicitly rebukes a youth-obsessed society that neither esteems nor intelligently employs its elderly.

"Old Mary," a cameo portrait of fortitude, declares, "My last defense / Is the present tense." The verb proclaims that her limited present gives her a kind of immortality. Complementing Old Mary's vigor, "The Crazy Woman" chooses to sing in November "a song of gray," recurrent hue of death and decay. Singing her ballad, flaunting conventional censure, she will not submit to an ageist pattern. "Crazy Woman" is capitalized as concept and person. Through her persona, the poet rejoices in a determined spirit that will praise life to the end.

"A Sunset of the City" compassionately depicts an aging woman alone. Emotionally dependent, facing empty later years, suicide enters her thoughts. Her monologue laments that children, husband, lovers, all view her as a relic of the past. "My daughters and sons have put me away with marbles and dolls" suggests the urban erosion of family life. "Indrying flowers of summer-gone" illustrates Brooks's compounding technique.

"On the Occasion of the Open-Air Formation / of the Olde Tymers' Walking and Nature Club" observes, with gentle amusement, the attempt of old people to recapture their childhood closeness to nature. Stately iambic pentameter and the title's antiquated spelling wryly comment on the proposed romp in the woods. The poet identifies with the old people ("we merry girls and men"), who may falter.

> —D. H. Melhem, "The Bean Eaters." *Gwendolyn Brooks: Poetry and the Heroic Voice.* (Lexington, Kentucky: The University Press of Kentucky, 1987): pp. 123-124.

MARIA K. MOOTRY ON PUBLIC RESPONSE TO *THE BEAN EATERS*

[Maria K. Mootry is assistant professor of black American studies at Southern Illinois University-Carbondale. She is widely published in journal such as *Obsidian, Phylon, College Language Association Journal, Massachusetts Review,* and *Open Places.* In this selection Mootry describes how the public responded to Brooks' collection of poems *The Bean Eaters* (1960) and explain the political and social atmosphere in the United States when the collection was published.]

When *The Bean Eaters*, Brooks's third collection of poetry, was published in 1960, America was beset by the upheaval of the civil rights movement. On the black American literary front, fiery spokesperson James Baldwin dissected and rebuked white Americans in his essays, while dramatist Lorraine Hansberry protested racial housing discrimination in the first Broadway play by a black woman, *A Raisin in the Sun* (1959). Brooks's audience, like that of Baldwin and Hansberry, was presumably white liberals, because many of the poems in *The Bean Eaters* originally appeared in major American magazines such as *Harper's, Poetry,* and *Voices.* Brooks's topical race themes, including the lynching of Emmett Till, Jr. in 1955 and the 1957 court-ordered integration of Arkansas schools, seemed to indicate that in the genre of poetry she assumed a poetic role parallel to that of Hansberry and Baldwin as witness and conscience for white America. But reactions to *The Bean Eaters* by that audience were oddly mixed.

Some reviewers found *The Bean Eaters* sufficient in content and form, while others found it too tame in its protest mission; still others were upset and put off by what they deemed an unseemly social emphasis. Thus, one reviewer pointed up the book's "deep compassion" and "concern for human misery," and another praised Brooks for touching on a "universal pattern of human suffering." But others denied the book's accessibility, accusing Brooks of a "complacent handling of . . . racial themes." Another group attacked Brooks's style as "an impressionistic method . . . too elliptical, private . . . and obscure," with the effect of making "social judgments difficult." Finally, some found *The Bean Eaters* a book of "disturbing overtones," presumably with reference to its social criticism.

In fact, according to Brooks herself, it was the "too social" quality of *The Bean Eaters* that frightened reviewers into an initial silence. Not "folksy" like her first volume, *A Street in Bronzeville* (1945), not "mandarin" like her second Pulitzer Prize–winning volume, *Annie Allen* (1949), *The Bean Eaters*, from its inception, presented a problem of interpretation for its critics.

One reason *The Bean Eaters* aroused such a range of disparate critical assessment was the way Brooks yoked her "social" message to a variety of classic high modernist techniques. By 1960, it should be remembered, the high modernism of Eliot, Pound, and Stevens was already paralleled by a burgeoning countermovement of postmodernism, sometimes labeled "personalism." Brooks, despite her social concerns, was temperamentally committed to the high-modernist concept of poetry impressed upon her as an apprentice writer (*Report*, 66–67). From this perspective, the duty of the modernist poet was to produce poetry that, in Richard Wilbur's words, "accommodates mixed feelings, clashing ideas, and incongruous images . . . the full discordancy of modern life and consciousness . . ." (Poulin, 460). Added to this was the tradition of distance between poet and poem, a tradition that downplayed the poet's own personality and assorted private demons, and demanded instead the type of "verbal scrupulosity" promoted by the New Criticism. In contrast, postmodernist poets of the late 1950s such as the black poet LeRoi Jones (now Imamu Baraka) and the female poet Sylvia Plath, spilled their "psychic guts" with unabashed forays into personal emotional suffering, while their contemporaries, the Beat poets, practiced other more social forms of personalism, with Ferlinghetti, Ginsberg, and others howling private/public jeremiads at America's sins.

Brooks avoided either extreme. If late modernists such as Plath and Baraka seemed obscure because of their poetry's inward biographical resonance, Brooks's obscurity rested on her meticulous craft. And if the visionary Beat poets were embarrassingly loud in their denunciations of America's social ills, Brooks was content with "disturbing undertones." Thus, Brooks located her rhetoric of social critique, her poetic discourse, in a range of studied poetic techniques, a *slanted* intentionality. This strategy allowed Brooks to "insinuate" her truths rather than to resort to the old-fashioned didacticism that, for many new critics, marred the work of her older contemporaries, such as then-poet-laureate Robert Frost. It equally allowed her to move beyond an entropic exclusive high-modernist "art for art's sake" aesthetic, and to do what her predecessor Emily Dickinson once advised: "Tell all the Truth, but tell it slant."

—Maria K. Mootry, "'Tell It Slant': Disguise and Discovery as Revisionist Poetic Discourse in *The Bean Eaters.*" *A Life Distilled: Gwendolyn Brooks, Her Poetry and Fiction.* eds. Maria K. Mootry and Gary Smith (Urbana, IL: University of Illinois Press, 1987): pp. 177- 179.

BEVERLY GUY-SHEFTALL ON ELDERLY WOMEN IN BROOKS'S POETRY

[In this extract, Guy-Sheftall discusses the manner in which Brooks's treats elderly women in her poetry.]

Brooks's urban world is also inhabited by older women who have a different kind of struggle. The persona in "A Sunset of the city" can be seen as a victim of a modern, urbanized environment, not necessarily Bronzeville, where close family ties have broken. She is resentful as she approaches middle age because of the way she is now treated by her children, husband, and lovers.

> Already I'm no longer looked at with lechery or love.
> My daughters and sons have put me away with marbles
>   and dolls,
> Are gone from the house.
> My husband and lovers are pleasant or somewhat polite
> And night is night.
>   (*WGB*, 337)

"Night is night" rather than a time for fun and adventure as it was when she was younger. Not only is it "summer-gone" where the seasons are concerned, but she is also approaching the winter of her own life. She is like the flowers and grass, which are personified.

> The sweet flowers indrying and dying down,
> The grasses forgetting their blaze and consenting to
>   brown.
>   (*WGB*, 337)

She sees herself as a hopeless woman whose needs are no longer satisfied in her cold, empty house.

> There is no warm house
> That is fitted with my need.
>
> I am cold in this cold house this house
> Whose washed echoes are tremulous down lost halls.
>   (*WGB*, 338)

Like old furniture, she is "dusty," and now "hurries through her prayers," because they seem useless. She contemplates suicide as an alternative to a numb existence where she would do nothing, feel nothing, and desire nothing. This death-in-life quality has been seen before in one of Brooks's women. The poem ends on a pessimistic note with her concluding that Fate has played a cruel joke on her. One critic sees this poem as "another indication of the spiritual bankruptcy of our times," of "the meaninglessness of modern living," and "our loss of faith." While the poem can be seen as having a universal theme, its central purpose should not be overlooked—the revelation of the inner turmoil of a woman as she faces a critical point in her life. The nature of the frustration she feels is in many ways different from what a man growing old would experience, yet similar.

Often Brooks's older women are seen in their relationships with their husbands, although these portraits tend to be less sharply focused than the ones that include a female figure only. In "the old marrieds" she explores, among other things, the negative impact of cramped ghetto quarters on a couple's relationship. Although the possibilities for romantic love have been perfect on this day, they are unable to communicate with each other because of circumstances beyond their control.

> And he had seen the lovers in the little side-streets.
> And she had heard the morning stories clogged with
>   sweets.
> It was quite a time for loving. It was midnight. It was
>   May.
> But in the crowding darkness not a word did they say.
>   (*WGB*, 3)

One would surmise that although it is dark, they still do not have the privacy desired for intimate contact. So, they remain silent. One might also conclude that the passage of time has caused their relationship to deteriorate to the point where it is impossible to express love.

In "The Bean Eaters," which also deals with an older married couple, Brooks explores the effect of poverty on their lives. They, like others in Bronzeville, attempt to make the most of their economic deprivation.

> They eat beans mostly, this old yellow pair.
> Dinner is a casual affair.
> Plain chipware on a plain and creaking wood,
> Tin flatware.
>   (*WGB*, 314)

Although they go about their daily lives in an almost mechanical manner, they refuse to give up.

> Two who are Mostly Good.
> Two who have lived their day,

> But keep on putting on their clothes
> And putting things away.
> (*WGB*, 314)

Their memories, some of which are unpleasant, keep their lives from being totally meaningless.

> Remembering, with twinklings and twinges,
> As they lean over the beans in their rented back room that
> is full of beads and receipts and dolls and cloths,
> tobacco crumbs, vases and fringes.
> (*WGB*, 314)

Although the couples in these two poems do have companionship, life seems to be just something to be endured. However the latter poem gives a more positive portrayal of the mates having endured together.

—Beverly Guy-Sheftall, "The Women of Bronzeville." *A Life Distilled: Gwendolyn Brooks, Her Poetry and Fiction*. eds. Maria K. Mootry and Gary Smith (Urbana, IL: University of Illinois Press, 1987): pp. 160-162.

MORT RICH ON THE COMMON LANGUAGE IN THE WORK

[Mort Rich is a professor at Montclair State University and a poet. He is an essayist who enjoys writing about poetry, critical thinking, and autobiography. In the following extract, Rich discusses how the language that Brooks uses in her poetry closely resembles the everyday language used by the people Brooks writes about.]

When Brooks wrote "a few hints" to younger writers about creating what she called "Black Poetry Writing," she suggested using "ordinary speech." Yet she also wrote, "Try telling the reader a little less . . . in a poem every word must work . . . not one word or piece of punctuation should be used which does not strengthen the poem." She reinforces this apparent contradiction in her ideas by writing, "loosen your rhythm so that it sounds like human talk. Human talk is not exact, is not precise. You must make your reader believe that what you say could be true." Brooks thus provides inconsistent or even contradictory criteria that may be used for examining her own poetry. What happens when these criteria are applied to "The Bean Eaters"?

Does the language of the poem read like inexact "human talk," or ordinary speech? Take, for instance, the lines "They eat beans mostly, this old yellow pair. / Dinner is a casual affair." The words are those of everyday language, but not so common is their order of presentation, which provides intensification through syntactic reversals of ordinary speech. A speaker might say, "This old yellow pair eats mostly beans," or, even closer to real speech, "this old couple." "Old yellow pair" resonates with connotations that are absent from "old couple." "Yellow," in the context of skin color, suggests faded, old, or the results of racial intermarriage; and "pair," more sympathetic than "couple," suggests connection—a mating for life. Thus, the first line sets a tone of affection and establishes the compassionate attitude of the speaker toward her subject. The author of *A Life of Gwendolyn Brooks*, George Kent believes that when Brooks wrote this poem, she was thinking of her elderly aunt and uncle who "could make a pound of beans go further than a pound of potatoes." The title, "The Bean Eaters", was inspired, he suggests, by Van Gogh's painting *The Potato Eaters*, that depicts an impoverished Flemish family barely subsisting on potatoes. (Readers are encouraged to look at reproductions of the painting and compare the feelings aroused to those generated by a reading of the poem.)

The line, "Dinner is a casual affair," like the first line, is not an ordinary statement. Though only five plain words, it is rich with implication. Beans are not usually associated with "dinner," a term that implies a formal eating situation; an irony is thus established that is fully realized with "casual affair." "Affair" implies a grand occasion, but that notion is contradicted by "casual," creating an oxymoron. The ironic tone is sustained for the rest of the stanza: "Plain chipware on a plain and creaking wood, / Tin flatware." "Chipware" is Brooks's own coinage, adapted from "dinnerware." Each word connotes a different world. "Dinnerware" implies wealth, privilege, and elegance, while "chipware" connotes old, cheap, worn-out dishes used by poor people; yet "chipware" also calls up the dignity of "dinnerware." The single word "chipware" thus leads a double life. "The plain and creaking wood," a metonymic way of saying "table," reinforces a sense of poverty, since no mention is made of a finely finished grain, or a tablecloth. The "creaking" is likely produced by loose or missing screws or nails, or glue so old it has dried and shrunk. Consistent with all of the previous images, "Tin flatware" is the cheapest available, though, like "chipware," the term implies its elegant counterpart, silverware. Like the old yellow pair, it is long-lasting, regardless of its initial cost.

This first stanza is also rich in sounds that express the denotations and connotations of their words. Three rounded "O" sounds offer a mouthful in the first line, followed by soft vowels in the second. These give way to harsher and more dominant consonant combinations in the third and fourth lines. "Tin flatware" almost imitates the sound of spoons and forks hitting plain wood. The repetition of "plain" lends emphasis to the scene represented and sets up a pattern of repetition seen in the next two stanzas.

The line "Two who are Mostly Good" may puzzle readers with its internal capitalizations. On a recording Brooks made of this poem, she does not seem especially to emphasize the two words. What, then, is implied? How different would the old pair appear if they were described as fully or genuinely good? Brooks seems to be making a concession to the idea that no one is completely good, even the old; their lives must be seen through the lens of "Mostly." In sound values, the line gives relief from the clattering "tin flatware" of the previous line, almost cooing with "Two who" and "Mostly Good." Thus sentimentality is introduced and the emotional atmosphere of the poem shifts. Brooks has followed her own advice by "telling the reader a little less" in this line, allowing the reader "to do a little digging." The next line, "Two who have lived their day," is a slant explanation or expansion of the vague judgment of the previous line. Living one's day may take many forms, some noble, some not. But, however they have lived, this pair now follows an ordinary routine of "putting on their clothes / And putting things away." In his book *Gwendolyn Brooks*, Harry Shaw suggests that their action is perfunctory, that "they are putting things away as if winding down an operation and readying for withdrawal from activity." The repetition of "putting" is the third repetition of a word within eight lines and creates an expectation that more repetitions will follow. They do, in the third (and last) stanza.

The lines "And remembering . . . / Remembering" takes repetition to the level of chanting, as if to imply a prayerful respect for the old pair. The ellipsis, unusual in poetry, breaks the meter of the poem, creating a unique space for the reader to enter these implied lives and ask, "What is forgotten?" The reader is not told what they remember, but instead how they recollect "with twinklings and twinges," a pair of words with an internal rhyme that twins almost contradictory feelings. Like "Mostly Good," "twinklings and twinges" has a push-pull quality—a giving and a taking way, or an illustrating by connotation and enacting through sound. These twin words offer alliterative echoes of youth, hope, and stars, contrasted with harsh memories and painful bodily feelings. The stanza then completes itself in what appears to be three lines of prose-like, ordinary speech. It is in fact, as Brooks says, a loosening of "rhythm so that it sounds like human talk."

The old pair's actions of eating beans and remembering are variations on acts of rumination that occur "As they lean over the beans." Harry Shaw proposes that the word "lean" suggests "a transcendence of a period of trouble," a specialized use of the word by Brooks which can be applied more broadly to the survival of black people. The stoic survival of this old couple, apparently in isolation, relies on a daily routine of nourishment supplied by minimal food and memories supported by "beads and receipts and dolls and cloths, / tobacco crumbs, vases and fringes." This random collection must be read as if sharing qualities with the earlier chipware and tin flatware; they are cheap household items that have been well used over the years. This collection, however, lacks any practical function in the couple's daily lives. Still, they are nourished by memories supported by this detritus of their past life as they persevere in their rented back room.

—Mort Rich, "Complexity in Plain Language: 'The Bean Eaters', by Gwendolyn Brooks." *Poetry for Students*, Gale, 1997.

B. J. BOLDEN ON POVERTY IN "THE BEAN EATERS"

[In this excerpt Bolden explains discusses the powerful way in which Brooks does not tell the reader that the old couple are poor; she hints at their poverty through metaphors and symbols.]

The undertone of poverty in this community of "bean eaters," which takes on the ambiance of class issues in the above two poems, flatly announces itself as economic deprivation in the poems "The Bean Eaters," "The Crazy Woman," and "A Lovely Love." Unlike the note of flippancy expressed by Langston Hughes' personae in "Ennui":

> It's such a
> bore
> Being always
> Poor. (*Selected Poems*, 131)

Brooks' depictions exude a note of melancholy over the fate of the ghetto dwellers:

> Two who are Mostly Good.
> Two who have lived their day,
> But keep on putting on their clothes
> And putting things away. (330)

Though "The Bean Eaters" is an apt portrayal of aging, as characterized by "this old yellow pair," it is also a social commentary on the dire poverty which has afflicted their lives in which home ownership, a goal of the American Dream, is not a genuine option for them; even in old age they have, not an apartment, but merely a "rented back room." The title poem of the book, *The Bean Eaters* is no casual romanticized reference to the aging of one Black couple; it is the report on the socioeconomic status of an entire Black community, evident in the opening quatrain:

> They eat beans mostly, this old yellow pair.
> Dinner is a casual affair.
> Plain chipware on a plain and creaking wood,
> Tin flatware. (330)

The beans eaten by this couple replicate the beans eaten by an entire community and are indicative of the meager economic resources of that community. The "Plain chipware on a plain and creaking wood, / Tin flatware" are the evidences of an entire life of "beans in their rented back room," while the memories of "with twinklings and twinges" admit to the joys, as well as sorrows of a life closing out with only "beads and receipts and dolls and cloths, / tobacco crumbs, vases and fringes" (330). By creating a vacillating metrical pattern, Brooks aligns the uneven economic straits of the couple's life to the formal structure of the poem. In the opening quatrain, she alternates the pentameter of the first and third lines with the tetrameter and trimeter of the second and fourth lines, followed by varied tetrameter and trimeter lines in the second quatrain. The final free verse stanza sprawls into uneven lines, enhanced by the rhetorical devices of anadiplosis and alliteration, and culminating in a catalogue of salvaged items "And remembering / Remembering" (330).

—B. J. Bolden, "The Bean Eaters (1960): Defining America." *Urban Rage in Bronzeville: Social Commentary in the Poetry of Gwendolyn Brooks*, 1945-1960, (Chicago: Third World Press, 1999): pp. 124-126.

CRITICAL ANALYSIS OF

"We Real Cool"

Of the plethora of poems written by Gwendolyn Brooks, "We Real Cool" is the most commonly anthologized. Although the poem consists of only eight lines, the tone, topic, word choice, and rhythm of the poem have made it a modern classic. The main theme in the poem is a bit bleak as it covers the activities of an unnamed "We" progressing from definitive statements like "We real cool" to descriptive statements like "We left school," and finally ending with the pessimistic prophecy "We die soon." Many critics have described the poem as a politically charged statement about the bleak future of African-American, inner-city youth. However, one could argue that it is just as likely to be a statement about the dim future that anyone who drops out of school may have.

At first glance, the poem's simple layout on the page suggests a simplicity in meaning. Upon a first reading, the poem appears to conceal little. The words are not difficult to understand independently, but it is not the words themselves that suggest deeper meaning. Rather, the context of the words in relationship to one another and the sequence of the full statements suggest contemplation.

The poem gains complexity through the interpretation of terms and speculations about the antecedent to the pronoun "We." To begin this investigation the first hint to the identification of this group of people is the subtitle of the poem " The Pool Players. Seven at the Golden Shovel." The subtitle suggests the possible location of the speaker and the group. It is somewhat stereotypical, but most people associate a pool hall with the activities and habits of less than desirable characters. Brooks's depiction of this unidentifiable we as a group who play pool is likely meant to create a negative tone in the poem. The second half of the subtitle adds equally intriguing information about this group. Once again the initial response is that of simplicity: "Seven at the Golden Shovel." The audience can hence deduce that the "We" referred to in the title are of group of seven pool players who frequent a club called the Golden Shovel. One of the intriguing things about Brooks's poetry is her attention to language choice and use. She does not arbitrarily assign words rather she carefully chooses the images that she wishes to portray in the poem. Her use of the number seven is not accidental and is actually one of the few positive references in the poem.

The number seven is often considered mystic or sacred. Babylonians and Egyptians list seven sacred plants to be used for healing; Ancient Greek historians have described an Arabian prayer ceremony beginning with covering seven rocks with blood; and Judeo-Christian religions indicate that there were seven days of creation, seven deadly sins, and seven sections in the Lord's Prayer. Further demonstration of the number's significance can be found in the Hebrews' praise of the seventh year as the year of sabbatical and the three great Jewish feasts last for seven days, while the Koran instructs Muslims that there are seven heavens, and there were seven wonders in the ancient world. Brooks ties into this mystical number by having seven pool players. It is a positive sign for the group, but Brooks uses the lucky number to show it takes more than luck for the group to survive in their world.

This group of seven is meeting at the Golden Shovel. Brooks, who uses a lot of color images in her poetry, often chooses her colors as references to something else. The shovel, a rather mundane tool that signifies death, is modified by the color golden. It's as if Brooks wants to point out that this shovel is unique or precious. However, at the same time, the term golden also carries with it overtones of old age, fall, and ripeness. Brooks's use of these two very specific words goes beyond the name of the bar to suggest the images of money and graves perhaps foreshadowing the early death of the pool players.

The title and the first line of the poem, "We real cool" sets the tone for the poem. Because this first line is in a colloquially spoken form that many critics have argued as resembling the slang of the African-American speech in the inner cities, Brooks's begins to narrow the subject matter down. The image of individuals at a pool hall engaging in speech and actions that are stereotypical of the behavior of individuals with a low educational level and low socioeconomic status is very powerful.

"We left school" is the only line in the poem that is in the past tense. In contrast to using the present tense, the past tense here implies a certain level of finality. In addition to the tense usage, Brooks's use of the verb left instead of quit or dropped out is ambiguous. We left school does not have to imply that the people dropped out of school permanently. The statement we left school can simply mean that at the end of the day this group left the school grounds. What is it about the line "We left school" that so strongly suggests that these individuals have dropped out of school permanently? The main factor contributing to that interpretation is the use of improper grammar throughout the poem. Every line of the poem is at best a simple sentence containing a subject and a predicate. The simplicity of the voice of the poem implies that the speaker is uneducated. Most interpretations of the poem suggest that the group has dropped out of school for good.

The third line begins to explain the time and location of the pool player's nocturnal activities. Once again there are many different ways to interpret the use of the verb. The fact that these players lurk late can be a straightforward description of their behaviors at the pool hall, but lurk implies a more devious meaning. It describes a person concealing their location before pouncing on someone. The use of the word lurk in conjunction with the word late suggests that this may also be the behavior of the players when they are not in the pool hall. In a similar manner Brooks allows for a dual interpretation with the "We Strike Straight."

To strike straight is a direct statement about the players' ability to hit billiard balls straight, suggesting they are accomplished pool players, but it can also be a description of their ability to hit, stab, shoot another person. They don't miss their targets. The next line of the poem describes their pride in their bad behavior. So proud, in fact, that they actually sing about their monstrous behavior. The statement reveals more than just this hubris, however, because it communicates to the audience that the players do have some sense of right and wrong. In order for them to "sing sin" they must first know what a sin is. In addition, singing about sin suggests a certain level of comfort with the sin because they are singing it to the world. The statements about sin are followed by a discussion of their intake of alcohol. The players thin gin. The probable use of the word thin here is to dilute something. A possible implication then is that the players enjoy drinking gin that has been diluted.

The next line is a statement about their musical taste or making fun of someone, but it could also be read as a statement about sexuality. The term jazz is often used in association with music, but it can also be used as an expression for making fun of someone or picking on them. With the capitalization of both Jazz and June both interpretations can be used. June could possibly refer to the month in which they enjoy listening to music or it could also be the name of a woman, June, who they enjoy making fun of. The final and darkest interpretation assumes that the word Jazz is a reference to sexual intercourse where the use of the pronoun We could imply some type of consensual sex with June or a horrific gang rape scenario. In either case, they don't seem to care about the ramifications of their behavior because they do not look into the future.

The final line in the poem abruptly ends the poem with a premonition about the players' deaths. The finality of the last line can then be placed as a justification for why they do all the other things that they do. There is little hope for the future, so they don't need school, they stay out late, they fight, they drink, and engage in sexual mischievous behavior. It does not matter because they will be dead soon.

"We Real Cool"

CLENORA F. HUDSON ON RACIAL THEMES

[Clenora F. Hudson is an essayist and critic. Her publications include *Africana Womanism: Reclaiming Ourselves, Emmett Till: The Sacrificial Lamb of Modern Civil Rights Movement, Contemporary Africana Theory and Thought.* In this extract, Hudson discusses how racial tension and generation gaps are discussed by Brooks in her poetry.]

The theme of "We Real Cool" is quite similar to that of "De Witt Williams" with its emphasis on the limitation of Black existence. One need only quote the poem itself to illustrate this point.

> We real cool. We
> Left school. We
>
> Lurk late. We
> Strike straight. We
>
> Sing sin. We
> Thin gin. We
>
> Jazz June. We
> Die soon. (p. 73)

To illustrate the suffering from violence the Blacks meekly endured in the past, "The Last Quatrain of the Ballad of Emmett Till" is an excellent example. Here the grief-stricken powerless mother is portrayed. The extent of her reaction is that: "She kisses her killed boy. And she is sorry" (81). Helplessly, she accepts the death of her son with foreknowledge that there is no recourse available to her to compensate for this tragic loss.

In "The *Chicago Defender* Sends a Man to Little Rock" two things are brought out. First the source of racism, which is primarily the insidious attitude of whites, is universal. Second, it is discovered that the lives of Blacks and whites in Little Rock epitomize the lives of people everywhere. Hence, "They are like people . . ." (89)

The Black experience is one of violence and stagnation. "The Ballad of Rudolph Reed" deals with the interrelationship between the two because it relates Rudolph Reed's attempt to extend beyond the stagnated limitations of his existence.

> "I am not hungry for berries.
> I am not hungry for bread.
> But hungry hungry for a house
> Where at night a man in bed
>
> "May never hear the plaster
> Stir as if in pain.
> May never hear the roaches
> Falling like fat rain . . . .
>
> All I know is I shall know it,
> And fight for it when I find it."

We are also given an account of the violent reaction of the whites to his aspiration,

> The first night, a rock, big as two fists.
> The second, a rock big as three . . . .
>
> The third night, a silvery ring of glass.

Trying to protect his home and family, Rudolph Reed was slain, and

> His neighbors gathered and kicked his corpse.
> "Nigger—" his neighbors said. (110–112)

The tragedy, of course, is that he was unsuccessful and this was/is in fact, the case with most Blacks.

Not only do Gwendolyn Brooks' poems deal with the mere existence of racism, but they also deal with the moods and attitudes created in Blacks as a result of racism. Among this group we have commentaries on the frustrated old Blacks and the fermentative youths. Dealing with the former, one need only look at "my dreams, my works, must wait till after hell" which deals with the frustrations of the Blacks, their dreams and their hopes.

> I hold my honey and I store my bread
> In little jars and cabinets of my will . . . .
> I am very hungry. I am incomplete.
> And none can tell when I may dine again.
> No man can give me any word but Wait,
> The puny light. I keep eyes pointed in . . . . (23)

In this poem one finds no indications of anger, unrest or any of the seeds of discontent so prominent in the young Blacks. Here we have a sense of helplessness, an attitude which suggests no control of one's life, or destiny. The ability to negotiate with life and all its responsibilities and problems is beyond reach.

Among the second group, involving the restless young Blacks, the poet records the passions and heat of the youths. The opening line of "Negro Hero" suggests this agitation: "I had to kick their law into their teeth in order to save them" (19). The young Blacks are excited, liberated, alive. They are defiant, and, in defiance, the spirit is rejuvenated. Hence, the youth says:

> . . . my blood was
> Boiling about in my head and straining and howling and
> singing me on. (P. 19)

This attitude is a marked contrast to that of the earlier generation of Blacks. Where there was emptiness, there is fulfillment; lack of confidence is replaced by arrogance, and fear is replaced by courage. Thus the youth continues: ". . . I am feeling well and settled in myself because I believe it was a good job . . ." (21)

In the poem "the progress" the fermentation of the youth is clearly illustrated. His awareness of the problem of racism, social hypocrisy, is presented. Note the lines:

> Still we applaud the President's voice and face.
> Still we remark on patriotism, sing,
> Salute the flag, thrill heavily, rejoice
> For death of men who too saluted, sang. (28–29)

As a consequence, ". . . inward grows a soberness, an awe, /A fear, a deepening hollow through the cold" (29).

Unlike the older Blacks, in "The Certainty we two shall meet by God" the youths do not accept dreams deferred, but rather they demand all of life's pains and pleasures, freedom and excitement, NOW!

> The Certainty we two shall meet by God
> In a wide Parlor, underneath a Light
> Of lights, come Sometime, is no ointment now.
> Because we two are worshipers of life,
> . . . We want nights

Of vague adventure, lips lax wet and warm,
Bees in the stomach, sweat across the brow. Now. (51)

They find no consolation in awaiting rewards in an afterlife but rather demand their rights to live their lives now.

The final poem to be discussed, "First fight. Then fiddle. Ply the slipping string" summarizes the moods of Black youth of today. The title, itself, is a cry for rebellion against repression, and the sonnet's closing lines capture this mood:

> . . . Rise bloody, maybe not too late
> For having first to civilize a space
> Wherein to play your violin with grace. (54)

Here we have a cry for reversing the order of sensibility—Passion over Reason. Hence, one must first fight for freedom and think about it after the battle is won.

There are other selections in Gwendolyn Brooks' volume of *Selected Poems* which comment on racism; however, from the ten discussed, it is obvious that her life and works were influenced by the existence of racism in America. They can serve as a chronicle of the moods, anxieties and pains of Blacks who were compelled to negotiate their lives with this almost unconquerable obstacle—racism—which engulfed them, warped them, and in some instances, destroyed them.

—Clenora F. Hudson. "Racial Themes in the Poetry of Gwendolyn Brooks." *CLA Journal* 17 (1972): pp. 17-20.

BARBARA B. SIMS ON THE SUBTEXT OF THE POEM

[Barbara B. Sims, executive director of the Metropolitan Community Center in Detroit, Michigan, is a critic who has published articles in *Mississippi Folklore Register, NMAL: Notes on Modern American Literature, Notes on Mississippi Writers*. In this brief explication of Brooks's poem, Sims outlines many of the possible metaphors used by Brooks and briefly discusses the meter of the poem.]

The economy of Gwendolyn Brooks' eight-line poem "We Real Cool" parallels the brevity of the lives of her subject, the pool players at the Golden Shovel. (. . .)

This one descriptive phrase conjures up an image of the black young male of the streets, lounging before the pool hall, shucking and jiving, dressed in a hip costume of colorful slacks, high-heeled boots, and Super-Fly hat, playing a transistor radio loudly. At this point the tone is one of self-congratulation, as if being "real cool" is where it's at. Of course, the players "left school."

The second stanza begins syntactically in the second line of the first couplet with the word "We," which is set curiously apart at the end of the line. The "We" is positioned as if to suggest that the identity of the players, individually and collectively, is less important than their traits and activities.

Stanza 2 tells that the players "lurk late" and "strike straight." The connotations of these phrases tell us that all the activities of the cool people are not as innocent as playing pool and hanging around the set. Mugging, theft, and rape, among other crimes, are suggested by the word "lurk," while "strike" is reminiscent of the gangland "hit," which signifies murder.

The cool people are proud of their way of life, however, for they "sing" (praise) sin. When they drink, they "thin gin" (gin and 7-up?). The final stanza refers to the players' interest in women—one of insincerity or playfulness. They "Jazz" June. Abruptly, Brooks concludes the poem: "We / Die soon."

Until the last line, the element of bravado in the diction and rhythm has made the activities of the street people seem somehow defensible, if not downright desirable. A certain pride in being outside the conventions, institutions, and legal structures of the predominant society is conveyed. Escaping the drudgery and dullness of school and work has left the lives of these drop-outs open to many romantic possibilities.

However, the tone changes dramatically when the reader learns the street people "Die soon." At once their defiant and complacent attitudes seem quite pathetic, and the reader wonders whom the cool people are trying to kid about the desirability of their disorderly lives.

—Barbara B. Sims, "Brooks's 'We Real Cool.'" *The Explicator* 34, 7 (1976): pp. 58.

[Patrick M. N. Stone has studied comparative and French literature, and has written on Victor Hugo, Beaudelaire, Marie de France, and Thomas Kyd. In this essay, he discusses the marginalization of "the players" through a framework of *jazzing*.]

For a poem so brief and said to be so unlabored, "We Real Cool" is deceptively powerful. As a drama of silenced voice, it achieves a taut unity through an intriguingly complex relationship with *jazzing*—at once *discussing* jazzing, *embodying* it, and *becoming* it. It is in this last facet, the *becoming*, that the poem locates its profound tragedy: through a chain of cause and effect, "the pool players" are denied access to self-expression. Their rejection of the expressive avenues of middle-class education establishes a "moral relationship" with that very middle class, which in turn leads to efforts at containment that rob the players' utterance of its strength. The universality of the "emasculation"—the poem's unique ability to communicate the inability to communicate—lends the work enormous value as an expression of disenfranchisement and marginalization.

Contextually, superficially, the term *jazzing* invokes both a habitual player-action and the syncopated, cool-jazz style of the versification; but its general sense is of a way of life in which energy is expended to create mood but not meaning. It is clear that, beyond their surly intensity and low-grade bravado, the players do have something to *say*. Their wordplay in their jazzing is self-conscious— the figure "Thin gin" makes an effort at cleverness, and "Jazz June" seems, poetically, to sacrifice meaning to assonance and alliteration. The poem embodies jazzing, then, linguistic and behavioral, to discuss it as a way of life without purpose. The tension between this undirected wit and "left school" implies that the players cannot be served by available institutions. "School" cannot accommodate their brand of intelligence.

Indeed, it may not *wish* to. The players have not internalized an importance of education, or the modes of self-expression it prescribes; and this disparity engenders the "moral relationship" cited by James D. Sullivan, between the middle-class privileging of formal education and the players' rejection of it. It is particularly astute of Gary Smith, then, to call the players' behavior "antisocial."

But Smith's term can pivot usefully: this is a poem about non-communication. Aside from an implied moral out-group, the text is addressed, spoken, *to* no one. Identity is consumed by no character internal to the text or projected by it. Even the stanzaic division effaces the players, its looseness heightening the sense of alienation. The short lines seem meek, as Sullivan suggests, huddled together on the vast page, and the players shrink into an expanse of not-them. Their victimization by printing convention was recognized in the Broadside edition of the poem (1966), which tried to free their viscerality from what Sullivan calls "the restrained silence of the printed page."

The "moral relationship" that colors both form and content thus contributes to the players' disintegration—to the *containment*, as Sullivan points out, of their "powerful rhythms" and "the sensual power of their discourse." Because they exist in and speak into the void, their "coolness" is lost, ineffectual. Even when the players claim to "[d]ie soon," they are meaninglessly, unconvincingly, generalizing the death experience. Left without climax, the utterance itself *becomes* jazzing, and it creates a detachment—that existential, appealing, "dis*order*ly" freedom cited by Barbara B. Sims—at once liberating and crushing. Sims contends that "the tone changes dramatically when the reader learns the street people 'Die soon'"; but the point is that its bleakness changes not at all.

Hortense Spillers is right, then: the poem summarizes the players' expectations, and thus their lives. Both the players and their speech act are bounded by context, and the expression is cropped, as Sullivan claims, by "the Procrustean bed of [middle-class] book design"—just as the players' opportunities are limited by cultural constraints. The meaning of the poem is in its jazz, its very meaninglessness, and the piece is dense with intimations of frustrated potency.

—This essay appears for the first time in this volume.

GARY SMITH ON REALITY VS. ROMANCE IN THE POEM

[Gary Smith is assistant professor of English at Southern Illinois University-Carbondale. His is an accomplished and respected researcher who has published numerous articles on Gwendolyn Brooks, Sterling Brown, Robert Hayden, and Melvin Tolson. In addition he is also a poet and has published one book of poetry, *Songs for My Fathers.* In this extract, Smith analyzes Brooks's balance between the reality of death and the youthful romantic approach the players in the poem have toward their lives.]

Perhaps no other poem by Gwendolyn Brooks has been as widely anthologized and generated as much critical debate as "We Real Cool." Much of the criticism questions why seven, presumably black, youths spend the substance of their lives in a wasteful antisocial manner. Also central to the poem is the debate over why Brooks chose to portray these lives in a poetic style that is at once romantic yet pathetically realistic.

To more than one critic, the answers lie in the sociopsychology of the pool players, themselves. For example, Eugene B. Redmond argues that, while the poem accurately conveys the jagged rhythms of jazz music and beat poetry, it also recites the "live-fast-die-young" syndrome of many urban black youths. Moreover, Barbara B. Sims suggests that the players' "defiant and complacent attitudes seem quite pathetic," and the reader wonders whom they are "trying to kid about the desirability of their disorderly lives."

What these interpretations overlook is the self-contained world of the poem. The pool players are *seven* personae, acutely aware of their mortal limitations ("We die soon") but immune to social criticism. According to Hortense Spillers, "they make no excuse for themselves and apparently invite no one else to do so." They *exist* in defiance of moral and social conformity and their own fate.

Below its surface realities, though, the poem is much more than a study in social pathology. Brooks's attitude toward the players remains ambivalent. To be sure, she dramatizes the tragic pathos in their lives, but she also stresses their existential freedom in the poem's *antibacchius* meter, the epigraph that frames the poem, and the players' self-conscious word play. (. . .)

The often overlooked epigraph to the poem suggests Brooks's ambivalence toward the personae's lifestyle. The number "seven," for example, ironically signifies their luck as pool players; while "golden" similarly implies a certain youthful arrogance. However, "shovel" reminds the reader of death and burial.

Within the poem, the personae's self-conscious word play supports their self-definition. The title, actually the first line of the poem, is a paradoxical understatement. As a colloquial expression, it boasts of the reason why the personae left school. This self-assertiveness centers on the word "real" that supplants the *to be* verb and modifies the predicate nominative "cool." The remainder of the sentences, while idiomatically correct—especially the second line, "We left school"—mock the value of education and celebrate the personae's street learning, Finally, the alliterative pattern of their other spoken words, "Lurk late," "Strike straight," and "Sing sin," belies any possibility for mental growth.

The most suggestive sentence in the poem, however, is "We Jazz June." Among its many meanings, the word "Jazz" connotes meaningless or empty talk and sexual intercourse. If the latter meaning is applied to the poem, "June" becomes a female or perhaps the summer of life whom the personae routinely seduce or rape; "die" thus acquires a double Elizabethan meaning of sexual climax and brevity of existence. Either connotation, obviously, works well within the players' self-appointed credo. More importantly, the rich word play suggests Brooks's own ambivalence toward the players' lifestyle. She dramatizes their existential choice of perilous defiance and nonconformity.

—Gary Smith, "Brooks's 'We Real Cool.'" *The Explicator* 43, 2(1985): pp. 49-50.

KATHRYNE V. LINDBERG ON THE "WE" IN "WE REAL COOL"

[In this extract, Lindberg discusses the ambiguous use of "We" in the poem. She also discusses the different possible audiences for the poem.]

Brooks's first Broadside broadside, "We Real Cool," whose title and refrain, borrowed from black English street argot, became something of an anthem, has an interesting history that makes Brooks a leader *avant la révolution,* if you will. Dudley Randall tells it, thus:

In May 1966, I attended the first Writers' Conference at Fisk University, and obtained permission from Robert Hayden, Melvin B. Tolson, and Margaret Walker, who were there, to use their poems.... I wrote to Gwendolyn Brooks and obtained her permission to use "We Real Cool." This first group of six Broadsides [is] called "Poems of the Negro Revolt."

Differently presented and received seven years after its publication in the collection *The Bean Eaters* (1960), Randall's broadside of Brooks's "We Real Cool" "was lettered white on black by Cledie Taylor to simulate scrawls on a blackboard," in keeping with the care he took to "harmonize . . . the poem, in paper, color, and typography." This is to say that Brooks's poem was afforded a place of distinction, if not literally a space on many a wall. This poem continues to generate interest, and, if only because I was at least surprised to see it treated to an apparently gratuitous dismissal in a recent issue of *Callaloo*, I would like to spend a few moments over it. Before rival readings, the poem, unfortunately *sans* graphics:

> We Real Cool
> > The Pool Players.
> > Seven at the Golden Shovel.
> We real cool. We
> Left school. We
>
> Lurk late. We
> Strike straight. We
>
> Sing sin. We
> Thin gin. We
>
> Jazz June. We
> Die soon.
>
> (*WGB*, 315)

Of this poem Hortense Spillers, praising the "wealth of implication" in this "[l]ess than lean poem," says it is "no nonsense at all." Finding original artistry, in-crowd and in-race code, and a full range of traditional poetic techniques in Brooks's poem, Spillers say that Brooks's players "subvert the romance of sociological pathos" and, quite comfortably, she has them read Brooks's lines, thus:

They make no excuse for themselves and apparently invite no one else to do so. The poem is their situation as they see it. In eight [could be nonstop] lines, here is their total destiny. Perhaps comic geniuses, they could well drink to this poem, making it a drinking/ revelry song.

I would like to bring Helen Vendler's recent mention of Brooks into conversation with Spillers's earlier tribute. Speaking with the well-earned authority of her position as a major reader of *the* Western canon and an influential critic of new poet candidates to that tradition, Vendler writes about the new national poet laureate in *Callaloo*, the most important wider-than-academic journal of black and Third World poetry. She generously praises and candidly corrects (explicitly *not* in the sense of "political correctness") the "Identity Markers" Rita Dove marshals to "confront . . . the enraging fact that the inescapable accusation of blackness becomes, too early for the child to resist it, a strong element of inner self-definition." At one point, Vendler economically dismisses Brooks in questioning one of Dove's "relatively unsuccessful historical excursions in a lyric time-machine." Not to make too much of a few lines, I quote her dismissal in full: "This [Dove's early 'odyssey'] may owe something to Gwendolyn Brooks's 'We Real Cool,' but it avoids the prudishness of Brooks's judgmental monologue, which though it is ostensibly spoken by adolescents, barely conceals its adult reproach of their behavior."

Even though Vendler indicates that Brooks's poem is not properly addressed to the white critical tradition, her response does not fail to register, however unwittingly, Brooks's double movement at once to narrow and to expand the usual distance readers of poetry traverse in becoming—or resisting becoming—"We," whether *real cool* or not. By making Brooks admonish the adolescents, Vendler makes pretty clear who isn't *We*—not to say who "We" isn't. It seems that, however fallen, Brooks, the poet, simply must share the critic's position above those pool players. Curiously, from their different aesthetic and experiential positions, Vendler and Spillers both give valid readings of the poem, and it is no accident that they fix on the pronoun that hangs out there like the prepositions from William Carlos Williams's famous wheelbarrow.

Not to dwell overlong on the ethos or impact of the very different constructions invited by Brooks's "We," I add Brooks's own commentary on the poem, which is delivered as stage directions for her public readings:

> First of all, let me tell you how that's ["We Real Cool"] supposed to be said, because there's a reason why I set it out as I did. These are people who are essentially saying, "Kilroy is here. We are." But they're a little uncertain of the strength of their identity. The "We"—you're supposed to stop after the "we" and think about *validity*, of course, there's no way for you to tell whether it should be said softly or not, I suppose, but I say it rather softly because I want to represent their basic uncertainty. (*RFPO*, 155–56)

Characteristically, Brooks invites both identification with and objectification of the young men—depending, perhaps on such categories as the race, gender, age of her/their audience. There is something cunning and deceptive both about the openness of Brooks's "We" and her variable distance from both the pool players to whom it refers and the people—at least since its Broadside republication—it seems to rename. Rather like the young white man who, in Brooks's story about Baraka, heeded a call not intended for him, or the "You" of "Primer for Blacks," that shifty pronoun works a critique on audience overidentification and poet's supposed representativeness. After all, isn't *she* supposed to correct the young punks, not to follow them as new leaders? But which *she*? The writer of "We Real Cool," *The Bean Eaters* (1960)? Or the writer of the 1967 broadside, "We Real Cool"? And should the differences of context and thus of content be *fixed*— either in the sense of "healed" or "halted"? Brooks put(s) her readers, specifically a black audience that is not limited to the no-longer-New Blacks of the sixties, to work on such questions.

—Kathryne V. Lindberg, "Whose Canon? Gwendolyn Brooks: Founder as the Center of the 'Margins.'" *Gendered Modernisms: American Women Poets and Their Readers*, eds. Margaret Dickie and Thomas Travisano (Philadelphia: University of Pennsylvania, 1996): pp 299-301.

[James D. Sullivan is an instructor in the English department at Illinois Central College, Peoria. He has been published in *Teaching English in the Two-Year College* and
wrote the book *On the Walls and in the Streets: American
Poetry Broadsides from the 1960's*. In the following selection, Sullivan discusses how the structure of the poem on
the page adds to the dramatic power of the poem.

Compare two presentations of "We Real Cool" by Gwendolyn
Brooks: first, the single most widely accessible edition of the poem,
on a page of her 1963 *Selected Poems* (73) published by Harper &
Row, and second on the 1966 broadside published by Broadside
Press. The words, in a formal linguistic sense, remain the same, but
the material presentation does not. Those physical qualities, as a
necessary condition for reading the poem, as an unavoidable part of
the thing read, create a different set of meanings in each artifact.

First, consider the book version, published before the emergence
of either Broadside Press or the Black Arts Movement. The poem
begins with an exposition of the dramatic context—the speakers and
setting in small capitals: "THE POOL PLAYERS. / SEVEN AT THE GOLDEN
SHOVEL." Their first dramatic line, "We real cool," repeats the title, a
complete Black English sentence, and it Suggests an interpretation
for what follows: these actions are manifestations or consequences
of coolness. The nonstandard grammar of the title and first line
transgresses the normal decorum of English language poetry, showing the social distance between the pool players and the middle-class
subjects of much of our poetic canon. The second sentence, "We /
Left school," establishes what I will call a moral relationship
between the players and the literate reader, buyer of poetry books.
This reader knows they shouldn't do that—knows better than they
do that this first manifestation of their coolness will surely harm
them, as it eventually does.

Beyond the collections of Brooks's poetry that include "We Real
Cool," however, this poem is even more widely available in teaching
anthologies at nearly all educational levels. Reception of the poem
within a school context, no matter what the class or racial make up

of the student body, would also likely encourage an interpretation that endorses education and condemns dropping out. Presented this text by an educational institution, students are likely to interpret it according to what they recognize as the values of that institution. For them, it is the school's own utterance. The tone of well-intentioned admonition from one of their elders might come across to the student readers in the way that Houston A. Baker Jr. reads it, as "an irony of loving kindness"—that repeated "We" working as an inclusive pronoun that forges a connection between these young people and the poet who sympathizes with them (27).

The simple, but strong and regular rhythm, reinforced by the jarringly nonstandard grammar, creates a sense of energy and aggressive physical power. But in the end, rhythm and syntax contain and finally cut off that vitality. The word "We" begins each short subject–predicate sentence and ends each line but the last. To maintain the syntactic pattern, the last line ends on the predicate, "Die soon," omitting the final "We." The predominant rhythm of the poem—two strong beats, one weak beat—resolve (satisfyingly) on the two strong beats in the last line. These two patterns, syntactic and rhythmic, converge to eliminate the final "We." The group dissolves in the last line, "Die soon," the final consequence of coolness, of energetically rejecting the middle-class respect for education. This satisfying little tragedy confirms the dominance and the rightness of values foreign to the players themselves. By the end they are completely powerless, dead.

The above paragraphs read "We Real Cool" as a poem about class relations, a theme difficult, especially if one knows the poet's other work, to separate from race relations. Given the political and social climate of the United States, a conjunction of race and class is inevitable. But what could all increased attention to visual design add to this reading? Can we find here a stronger value in the whiteness of the paper and the blackness of the ink than in "Ballad of Birmingham"? Perhaps a metaphorical reading of color in the smallness of the black poem as against the expanse of white paper? Can we find a critique of humanist assumptions in whiteness as a universal standard of legible space—ubiquitous, non-contingent whiteness—and black as a differentiation upon it? The very conventionality of the white page denies that it carries any such meaning. It is, by convention, merely conveniently available for any inscription. Because of this resistance, any reading of the paper and the ink calls for more than simple metaphoric correspondences.

The elegance of the typeface and the evenness of the layout in *Selected Poems* are products of craftsmanship, so well produced that they are refined out of notice. That particular grace and craft are from a world outside the pool hall. The pool hall demands an accuracy of its own ("We / Strike straight"), but it is not the accuracy of precisely tooled finials and even leading. The speech is first person, but the studied aesthetics of the type does not emerge from the aesthetic values of the pool-playing dropouts who are supposedly speaking. The publisher, or the book designer Cy Axelrad, quotes their discourse, speaks their words to the readers, images their language through a mainstream graphic vocabulary and thus presents it with what Mikhail Bakhtin would call a new "accent." The conventions of commercial publishing demand that the poem appear in such a decorous format. This is the work of "a distinguished modern poet, recipient of the Pulitzer Prize," as the back-cover blurb of the paperback edition says, and the dignity of the format befits the dignity of that status. All this is part of the marketing strategy for the book, and everything a potential purchaser might see in the artifact prior to reading it must be subordinate to the limits of that strategy. The alternative aesthetic of pool hall cool in the language of the poem thus is reshaped to fit the Procrustean bed of book design. The (aesthetic) values of the (white) middle class prevail.

The broadside version appeared in 1966, when Brooks was becoming more radically engaged in racial politics. Broadside Press was an emerging institution within the new Black Arts Movement, and Randall intended his publications for distribution, more specifically than did Harper & Row, to African American readers. The design inverts the most pervasive printing convention of all into white lettering on a black field. This particular field is not a given, as a white field is when it appears as an already white sheet of paper. It is contingent. The uneven brushwork that made this black field (on a white sheet) remains visible, uneven at the edges. This is not the even, neutral, potentially infinite space of the white page; here the field of discourse is itself the inked intrusion. The lettering is not a matter of shaped ink forming legible symbols against a contrasting passive medium: the letters are negative space, gaps in the field, shapes made by the field itself; the ink still forms the shapes, but the material seen in the letter is now the paper. Language clears space in that field, exposing the white surface rather than concealing it. By creating an unconventional relationship between ink and paper, this broadside makes that relationship legible. It raises the question of whether that more conventional book page works any differently, whether the familiar habits of book design are any less contingent in their composition or more innocent of meaning themselves. It becomes reasonable to see the setting in which this discourse is quoted as a specifically—and literally—black setting in the one case and white setting in the other.

The conventions of English language texts privilege the top of the page, The eye begins to read there and reads the words below in terms of that prior rhetorical context. As a verbal text, the broadside "We Real Cool" privileges the title, byline, and dramatic exposition in that way by placing them at the top, but it prints them in smaller letters than the body of the poem. Considered as an image also rather than only as a poem, it privileges the large figures in the center, the letters that represent the speech of the pool players; the small figures above and below—the otherwise controlling dramatic, literary, and publishing context—are subordinate.

It looks like either a chalkboard or graffiti. The refined transparencies of classic typography and the printed, bound pages of a well-produced hardcover book would not be available for these pool players to use to speak for themselves. As chalkboard writing, it appears in a setting familiar, if uncongenial, to the pool players. These are the rough letters they can make themselves in order to speak in a setting that has been available to them. Appearing thus so brazenly in the school setting that the pool players themselves have rejected, this text is an empowering nose-thumbing at the institution that had once controlled and restricted them—thus, also, a rejection of the school-values that would interpret the poem as an endorsement of education. As graffiti, the poem is an anonymous, unregulated, transgressive utterance, not the work of that contained, knowable, critically manageable construction, the imagination of the poet. It is a rebellious sort of folk culture. Coming in from the suburbs, I recognize that it belongs here, and I don't. In either case, chalkboard or graffiti, although it is still a setting produced by a publisher and a designer, it is neater than the book design is to something the anony-mous pool players could produce for themselves. Broadside Press quotes the players' discourse, but in a manner that respects and assents to their own accent.

The transgressive power of the poem is no longer contained in a banal tragedy of uneducated inner city youth. Cledie Taylor's graph-ic design for the broadside frees the powerful rhythms from their conflict with the restrained silence of the printed page, recovering the sensual power of their discourse not in imagined rhythms but in real visual effects. The printed word in the book, though it cannot entirely suppress the rhythmic force of the poem, still presents the poem as a passive object for the reader's intellectual contemplation. In such a clean setting, middle-class readers can find comfort in their superior moral relation to the dropouts, whose physical, sensual presence they need not confront. Taylor's design for the broadside makes their discourse sensually aggressive, even heroic.

—James D. Sullivan, "Real Cool Pages: The Broadside Press Broadside Series and the Black Arts Movement." *On the Walls and in the Streets: American Poetry Broadsides from the 1960's*, (Urbana: University of Illinois Press, 1997) pp. 33-38.

"Bronzeville Woman in a Red Hat"

The title of this poem is a reference to Brooks's first collection of poetry *A Street in Bronzeville* (1945). Bronzeville is a predominately African American suburb of Chicago where Brooks grew up. Although this particular poem does not appear in that first collection, Brooks uses the reference to her earlier work and the suburb Bronzeville to provide descriptive background about the woman wearing a red hat. Based on the types of poems in *A Street in Bronzeville* the woman is most likely an elderly African-American woman and probably a caricature of someone Brooks knows. Many of the poems in that collection describe the ordinary, daily activities of the people living in that part of town. Poems such as "The Mother," "Queen of the Blues," "The Old Marrieds," and "Sadie and Maud" are representative of the partly autobiographical themes found in her first collection. The poem "Bronzeville Woman in a Red Hat" is from the book *The Bean Eaters* (1960), a collection that contains many of Brooks's most well known poems including the title poem "The Bean Eaters" and "We Real Cool."

The basic theme of the poem is the hiring of an African American housekeeper by a prejudice white family. The unraveling of this story is broken into two sections. The first part of the poem is the introduction of the White family to an African American woman who is applying for a job as a housecleaner or cook for the family. In addition, Brooks uses this opportunity to explain what happened to the previous housecleaner. The second portion of the poem is the description of one instance where the housekeeper tends to the needs of one of the young children in the house and how the mother of the child reacts to this care.

The first line of the poem sets up some vague references "They had never had one in the house before." Through careful reading of the next lines is it possible to determine that the antecedent of the pronoun, "they," is an upper class white family. The vague introduction continues with the addition of the indefinite pronoun "one." If a comparison is made between the title and the first line, then the use of the pronoun "one" can either be the "Bronzeville Woman" or "a

Red Hat." The interesting sentiment created by Brooks is that to the family this woman has the same if not less humanity than the hat with which she is adorned. The dehumanizing tirade continues with a litany of comparisons between the woman and a lion, puma, panther, and black bear.

Brooks creates an image of the white family or at least the "mistress" of the house looking in disgust at a black woman standing at the threshold of her front door. The African-American woman is not really human to them until they notice the hat—her features becoming more human and "refreshing." Only the civility of a woman wearing a red hat can battle against the "semi-assault of that extraordinary blackness." Once the hat has been identified as a qualifying human characteristic, Brooks begins to identify some traces of humanity in the other features. Even under this gradual acceptance of humanity, the narrator of the poem describes the family's negative reaction to the slackness of the woman's pink mouth and the worn and battered look of her eyes. The momentary human reaction to the woman is immediately dashed to the ground when the narrator belittles any sympathy to the woman's difficult life and explains that the mistress should not have these types of emotions for "…her slave…." This introductory stanza ends with the return to the opening line of the poem giving the impression of how quickly the scene had taken place.

The next stanza abruptly switches to the explanation of who the Mistress is, Mrs. Miles (an ironic anagram spelling Smile), and why her old cook, Patsy Houlihan, had left Mrs. Miles's employment. Furthermore, Brooks uses these lines as a way of demonstrating just how despicable Mrs. Miles is. A gruesome tale is told of the death of Patsy Houlihan's daughter at the hands of Patsy's deranged husband, and the only thing on Mrs. Miles's mind is the completion of her biscuits, curry, soup and salad. Mrs. Miles has no compassion for her cook's family. This first section of the poem then concludes with the explanation of what led the African-American woman to Mrs. Miles' kitchen.

In the second part of the poem, Brooks describes the mistresses's reaction to the woman coming to the aid of her child. The event Brooks creates is either a real event occurring in the Miles's household or an event happening in Mrs. Miles's mind as she interviews the Bronzeville woman in the red hat. Whether these events are happening in real time, the future, or in Mrs. Miles' imagination, Brooks allows the reader to peer inside the prejudice world of Mrs. Miles. The scene is of the cook coming to the aid of one of Mrs. Miles's children who has injured him or herself. The narrator has an omnipotent understanding of Mrs. Miles here and the reader is allowed to hear Mrs. Miles' thoughts as she sees "the black maid" kiss her "creamy child." Mrs. Miles's racist hatred outweighs her logic, and she sees the maid as an animal preying on her child instead of a concerned human trying to comfort a distressed and injured child.

The next stanza reveals the thoughts of the injured child who is looking for comfort, or "human humoring." Then the child relaxes, and the maid takes care of him or her. Her kiss is "honey upon marvelous grime." This child's pains are diminished, and Brooks hints that the curing power of the maid does more than just make the child's physical pain subside, but that it also breaks apart the monster of prejudice allowing the child to see the maid for the person that she is and not the monster that Mrs. Miles has made her out to be. This change in the child's perception is further elaborated in the following stanza where Mrs. Miles tries to take her child from the Bronzeville woman.

She wants to take away any impurity that the child has been infected with and "pry the ordure [excrement] from the cream." She attempts to lure her child from the "cannibal wilderness" of the Bronzeville woman's arms and bring him or her into the "sun and bloomful air" of her prejudice white world. The drama of this situation is further developed when the child defiantly refuses to return back to his or her mother. Moreover, the child returns the maid's affection and reciprocates the kiss. The final stanza describes the absolute horror that Mrs. Miles feels as she watches the Bronzeville Woman take care of her child.

"Bronzeville Woman in a Red Hat"

BEVERLY GUY-SHEFTALL ON THE MEANING OF
"BRONZEVILLE WOMAN"

[In this extract, Guy-Sheftall discusses the characteristics
and attitudes of the Bronzeville Women in Brooks's poetry.]

Although one might disagree with this assessment of her as a woman
writer, it is difficult to ignore her numerous portraits of the women
who inhabit Bronzeville, the setting for much of her poetry.

Like Richard Wright, she explores the tragic aspects of black
ghetto life, but she also probes beneath the surface in order to illuminate those areas of the slum dweller's life that often go unnoticed
and should not be seen as ugly or horrifying. Ironically, then, her
poems reveal both the destructive and the nurturing aspects of the
black urban environment. Brooks's paradoxical vision is perhaps
best revealed in a statement concerning her plans for *In the Mecca*
that appears in the appendix of her autobiography.

> I wish to present a large variety of personalities against a mosaic
> of daily affairs, recognizing that the *grimmest* of these is likely to have a
> streak or two streaks of sun.
> In the Mecca were murders, loves, lonelinesses, hates, jealousies.
> Hope occurred, and charity, sainthood, glory, shame, despair, fear,
> altruism.
> (*Report,* 189–90)

A central paradox of her composite portrait of Bronzeville is the
ability of its residents to transcend, if only temporarily, the sordid
conditions of their lives. They are not dehumanized or paralyzed by
the poverty that engulfs them. It is against this backdrop of Brooks's
overall vision of Bronzeville that her images of urban women as they
appear in selected poems from *The World of Gwendolyn Brooks* will
be examined. Although a discussion of the urban woman in *In the
Mecca*, *Riot*, and *Family Pictures* will not be included, it would be
interesting in a more comprehensive study of Brooks's women to
compare the images projected in her pre-1967 poems with these later
ones.

The diverse nature of Brooks's females enables her to reveal the many facets, complexities, and paradoxes of the urban black experience. They range from the death-in-life figure of a woman in "obituary for a living lady" to the life-in-death figure of a woman in "the rites for Cousin Vit." The unnamed woman in the first poem, based on a person Brooks knew well (*Report*, 154), is the antithesis of Cousin Vit. Although she was a "decently wild child" and as a girl was "interested in a brooch and pink powder and a curl," as a young woman she would not permit sexual contact between herself and the man with whom she had fallen in love. She continued to wait by the windows in a "gay (though white) dress," and finally decided to say "yes," although by this time it was too late because he had found a woman "who dressed in red." Although red traditionally has negative connotations where women's dress is concerned, here it is being used positively to contrast the latter woman's *joie de vivre* with the lack of it in the main character; her purity and paleness of spirit (which the white dress symbolizes) cause her to be rejected. Here Brooks has taken the conventional "scarlet woman" figure usually associated with the corrupt, sinful city and transformed her into a positive, vital force. After mourning for a long time and "wishing she were dead," the woman in white turns to religion and away from the world of the flesh.

> . . . Now she will not dance
> And she thinks not the thinnest thought of any type of
> romance
> And I can't get her to take a touch of the best cream
> cologne.
> (*WGB*, 18–19)

Cousin Vit, on the other hand, has lived an exciting, full life and even in death refuses to be confined.

> . . . it can't hold her,
> That stuff and satin aiming to enfold her . . .
> . . . Even now, surmise,
> She rises in the sunshine. There she goes,
> Back to the bars she knew and the repose
> In love-rooms and the things in people's eyes.
> Too vital and too squeaking . . . .
> (*WGB*, 109)

She has tasted much of life's pleasures and sorrows. Disappointments have not caused her to withdraw from life and miss out on its more pleasant aspects.

> Even now she does the snake-hips with a hiss,
> Slops the bad wine across her shantung, talks
> Of pregnancy, guitars and bridgework, walks
> In parks or alleys, comes haply on the verge
> Of happiness, . . .
>
> (*WGB*, 109)

She has taken chances in order to find joy. Ironically, she seems more alive in death than the living woman in the previous poem. One critic has commented on her and other women in Brooks's poems who are to be admired for attempting to get the most out of their basically narrow and drab lives.

> Whatever her shortcomings, Cousin Vit has asserted her pagan self without asking questions or whining. It may be that she, Sadie, and others like them, girls who "scraped life/With a fine-tooth comb," girls who seize their love in hallways and alleys and other unconventional places—it may be that these carefree souls have a deeper understanding of the modern scene than any of their sedate sisters and friends. Perhaps they are the only ones who do understand.

"Sadie and Maud" (alluded to in the previous quote) deals with two sisters whose contrasting approaches to life are somewhat analogous to the women discussed in the two previous poems. Sadie, like Cousin Vit, has gotten out of life all it has to offer, despite her limited resources.

> Sadie scraped life
> With a fine-tooth comb.
>
> She didn't leave a tangle in.
> Her comb found every strand.
> Sadie was one of the livingest chits
> In all the land.
>
> (*WGB*, 16)

Although she bore two illegitimate daughters and shamed her family, she has left her offspring a rich heritage—her fine-tooth comb—

so that they will presumably also squeeze as much joy out of life as possible. She does not have wealth to leave them, but she leaves them something perhaps equally valuable. Maud, on the other hand, who followed the more conventional path and went to college, is, at the end of the poem, alone and like a "thin brown mouse." Like the unnamed woman in "obituary for a living lady," she has followed society's rules, but her life has lacked the vitality and fullness that makes one's existence meaningful.

—Beverly Guy-Sheftall, "The Women of Bronzeville." *A Life Distilled: Gwendolyn Brooks, Her Poetry and Fiction*, eds. Maria K. Mootry and Gary Smith (Urbana, IL: University of Illinois Press, 1987): pp. 153-156.

D.H. MELHEM ON BROOKS'S VOICE IN THE POEM

[In this brief extract Melhem provides a brief description of the sarcastic voice used in the poem.]

"Bronzeville Woman in a Red Hat" registers passionate feelings in the color itself. One recalls that Brooks had worked briefly as a maid. The subhead, "Hires Out to Mrs. Miles," indicates both occupation of the employee and status of the housewife, implying the distance (miles) between them.

The poet's heavily sarcastic voice refers to the worker as a "slave." The poem satirizes the white woman's repugnance when her child is kissed by the black woman and kisses her in return. Mrs. Miles translates natural acceptance into "unnatural" animal wildness. For her, "nature" perversely roots in convention and prejudice. A two-part work, the poem's closing quatrain's *a b b a*, outer rhymes containing the inner two, suggests the reciprocated embrace. Division of the piece paradoxically indicates both separation (color, class) and, in the second part, pairing by natural affection. The child's response to the black woman (emergency replacement for an underpaid Irishwoman) conveys some optimism. Generic names ("child," "big black woman," "Bronzeville Woman," etc.) signal allegory. As in "Jessie Mitchell's Mother", the young offer hope for improving society.

—D. H. Melhem, "The Bean Eaters." In *Gwendolyn Brooks: Poetry and the Heroic Voice*, (Lexington, Kentucky: The University Press of Kentucky, 1987): pp. 121.

RICHARD FLYNN ON CHILDREN IN BROOKS' POETRY

[Richard Flynn is a professor of Literature at Georgia Southern University. He is an accomplished critic and activist who worked as a law clerk for Chief Justice Earl Warren on the famous court case ending segregation, *Brown v. Board of Education*. In this selection, Flynn explains the importance of children in Brooks's poetry as metaphors for hope and change in the future.]

In the '50s, Brooks wrote as a young mother whose poetry was essential for the well-being of her own children in a racist society; today, she writes as a poet with decades of a political commitment to working closely with children and poetry. In her work of the '60s and '70s, Brooks's children are catalysts for change, both as symbols and through their own poetic voices: The remembered "infant softness" of Emmett Till becomes a symbol that awakens the conscience of the Mississippi mother for whose sake he has been lynched ("A Bronzeville Mother Loiters in Mississippi. Meanwhile, a Mississippi Mother Burns Bacon," *Blacks* 333–39), while the voice of the murdered Pepita S. in her couplet at the end of "In the Mecca" ("I touch"—she said once—"petals of a rose. A silky feeling through me goes!" [*Blacks,* 433]) "becomes the most vital voice of the community," as Gayl Jones (203) points out. By 1975, Brooks had become increasingly concerned with fostering children's vital voices, so that rather than being "offered in distorted images through the mirrors of others," as Jones says of Pepita, they may "speak for [themselves]" (203). In her *ars poetica*, published in a capsule course in *Black Poetry Writing* (1975), Brooks instructs novice writers to "Remember that ART is refining and evocative translation of the materials of the world!" (Brooks et al., 11) and calls for "a new black literature" that will "italicize black identity, black solidarity, black self-possession, and self-address" (3).

—Richard Flynn, "'The Kindergarten of Consciousness': Gwendolyn Brooks and the Social Construction of Childhood." *African American Review* 34, 3 (2000): pp. 492-493.

B. J. Bolden on Economic Deprivation in the Poem

[In this excerpt Bolden discusses the connections between socioeconomic status and racial relation in the poem.]

"Bronzeville Woman in a Red Hat" once again returns to the theme of economic deprivation as an adjunct to social inequality as evidenced by the subheading "Hires out to Mrs. Miles" which not only distances the domestic servant from her "wage-paying mistress," but further establishes her lack of importance and parallel lack of individual identity (367). Though the title vaguely references any Bronzeville woman, it paradoxically limits and distinguishes this particular woman by its allusion to her "red hat." The symbolism inherent in the ironic referral to her red hat provides an alternative view of a Black woman as a domestic, versus one whose private life speaks to more vibrant, independent, and sassy inclinations. Like Hattie Scott, in "the end of the day" and "at the hair-dressers" (*A Street in Bronzeville*, 51, 53), the woman's red hat signals a well-established life counterpoised against the financial and physical constraints of life as a domestic.

The radiant energy innate to the meaning of red is also apparent in poems by both Langston Hughes and Sterling Brown. In "When Sue Wears Red," Hughes hails Susanna Jones whose red dress is indicative of her "beauty," while in "To Sallie, Walking," Brown similarly complements the "vividness" of Sallie, who, when she walks, is "provocative, discreet." Yet ultimately, by contrast, this same "red," suggestive of vibrant life, will eventually inform the violence of lynching in "A Bronzeville Mother" and "The Last Quatrain of the Ballad of Emmett Till."

The menial domestic role of the Bronzeville woman is a role that has been common to working class Black women, both in the South, since the days of slavery, and in the North, since the days of the Great Migration. Brooks' use of free verse and a random line structure addresses the lack of rhyme or reason in Mrs. Miles' first attributing the animalistic traits of "A lion, really. Poised / To pounce. A Puma. A panther. A black / Bear," to a human being then, though ambivalent, entrusting the care of "her creamy child" to such a "creature" (367). The first verse pointedly signifies the woman as subhuman in the lines, "They had never had one in the house before," and "There it stood in the door" (367). And rather than concede to the attractiveness of the red hat, which is clearly informed by an unfamiliar culture, Mrs. Miles labels the hat "rash, but refreshing— / In a tasteless way, of course." She is duly offended by the "dull dare, / The semi-assault of that extraordinary blackness" of her slave" (367).

The second verse of the two-part poem permits a recognition of the fact that Mrs. Miles' seemingly disparate racial views are not limited to Black people, but a dual statement on racism and classism, since she holds a diminished view of her Irish housekeeper's humanity as well. Though Patsy Houlihan's absenteeism is a result of the tragic events surrounding the murder of her daughter, that fact countenances no sympathy on the part of "mistress" Miles. Instead, her need for "the biscuit blending," "the curry," "soup," and "tossed salad" steer her thoughts to Mrs. Houlihan's inconsiderate ways, but not to her own inhumanity. Grammatically, the Black maid is labeled a nonhuman entity in the final lines of part 1:

> The Alert Agency had leafed through its files—
> On short notice could offer
> Only this dusky duffer
> That now made its way to her kitchen and sat on her
> kitchen stool. (369)

The references to her as "that" and "it," rather than the human "who," set the stage with a backdrop for Mrs. Miles' horror at having a "beast," not a person, kiss her white child, whose finger is bleeding and who longs for some "human humoring" (369).

But ironically, the white child's affinity for the Black maid, far from being the world-shaking event which defines his mother's reaction, is for him a show of affection in a world otherwise peopled by his mother, whom the Irish woman labels "'Inhuman.' And 'a fool.' / And 'a cool One.'" Though Mrs. Miles is filled with "disgust" at the intimacy of the act and senses that she has been deprived of a valuable possession, which she tries to extricate or "pry the ordure from the cream," the child resists with an emphatic "No," and "Kissed back the colored maid" after becoming "Conscious of kindness, easy creature bond" (369).

Brooks' poem recalls a similar scenario in Ann Petry's *The Street* (1946). The poverty-stricken protagonist, Lutie Johnson, notes in this stream-of-consciousness narrative that "she'd cleaned another woman's house and looked after another woman's child while her own marriage went to pot ..." (30). Indeed, in a contextual structure nearly parallel to "Bronzeville Woman in a Red Hat," Lutie arrives at the interview for a domestic position in "high-heeled shoes and thin stockings and this wide-brimmed hat" quite in contrast to the "ribbed stockings made of very fine cotton and flat-heeled moccasins . . . and no hat" of her mistress-to-be (36). Similarly, Lutie is placed in charge of a white child who was "just a nice, happy kid, liking her at once, always wanting to be with her" (39). And the same "coolness" evident in the character of Mrs. Miles, likewise frames the profile of Lutie's mistress: "She wasn't too sure that Mrs. Chandler was over fond of Little Henry; she never held him on her lap or picked him up and cuddled him the way mothers do their children. She was always pushing him away from her" (39).

This close bond between Black domestic workers and the white children they tended is the focus of an article, "Say Dixie Whites Are Not Bad Folks," by Lew Sadler. As he elucidates some of the social norms and the "good neighbor" codes existing between Southern Blacks and whites, Sadler highlights discernible evidence of Blacks in the lives of whites:

My wife was raised by a Negro woman, as have so many other ladies of the south. That still is the case. You can drive by our parks and yards and see how many white children are cared for by, not white nurses, but colored women . . .

I've seen many times the mother come home from work, and the kids would hold on to the Negro woman's legs letting themselves be dragged to the sidewalk and on into the car before letting go, because they didn't want her to leave. Does that look like we are allergic to Negroes? (Williams, 55)

Sadler's perspective establishes the Southern origins of the Black woman as primary caretaker to the white child and recalls the days of slavery when, among many domestic roles the Black woman held, nurturing her mistress' children was deemed more critical than caring for her own. Thus, although the poem suggests a Northern environment, it also recalls the transmission of the Southern social codes, which were transplanted along with the Southern Blacks who migrated north in hopes of social equality.

The lack of humanity accorded Black Americans, as depicted in the poem, "Bronzeville Woman in a Red Hat," is also reflective of America's persistent predilection for violence where Blacks are concerned. As Brooks' voice urges toward the political in the poem "In Emanuel's Nightmare: Another Coming of Christ," the allusion to violence, though subtle, is distinctly evident in terms of defining America. A historical perspective of the social climate of the years 1945–1960, the period covered by Brooks' first three works, bears out white America's abiding potential for violence, directed at both their fellow Black citizens at home, as well as their engagements in World War I and World War II.

—B. J. Bolden, "The Bean Eaters (1960): Defining America." *Urban Rage in Bronzeville: Social Commentary in the Poetry of Gwendolyn Brooks*, 1945-1960, (Chicago: Third World Press, 1999): pp. 134-138.

"Riot"

One of the most powerful and political poems written by Gwendolyn Brooks is the poem "Riot." This poem was written during what most critics associate with the beginning of Brooks's political works. Her poetry took a dramatic turn in 1967 after watching LeRoy Jones (Amiri Baraka) and other Black Nationalists speak at Fisk University. It was a turning point in her life marked by a few collections of her poetry: *The Wall (1967) and In the Mecca (1968)*. After the assassination of Martin Luther King Jr. in 1968, the country was shocked, and protests and gatherings sprung up around the country and Chicago was not an exception. The poem Riot is a direct response to the events following the assassination.

The poem is divided into three parts with each part covering the past, present, and hopeful future of social equality respectively. Brooks uses the events and people surrounding an actual riot that occurred in Chicago. The three sections are subtitled, "Riot," "The Third Sermon on the Warpland," and "An Aspect of Love, Alive in the Ice and Fire" Respectively. "Riot" describes a single incident occurring in the past with John Cabot as the figure representing the status quo of social equality. "The Third Sermon on the Warpland" describes the current state of social unrest about racial inequality in the United States and is told through a descriptive third person narrative as a riot is taking place. The final part of the poem, "An Aspect of Love, Alive in the Ice and Fire" is a song of hope for the future of the civil rights movements and describes the feelings of the protesters during and after the riot.

In "Riot" Brooks chooses to use the image of John Cabot, the Italian explorer credited with the discovery of North America, to address the historical oppression of African Americans. His racist attitude toward people of color and his ethnocentric view of any culture other than his own make him the perfect representative of oppressive behavior.

Brooks begins the poem with an epitaph from Martin Luther King Jr. to set the tone for the poem. Brooks uses King's quote "A riot is the language of the unheard" in connection with John Cabot to explain why riots have occurred in the past, and why riots still occur.

The poem begins with a description of John Cabot. Through a list of things that Cabot uses to define himself, Brooks explains that Cabot refuses to acknowledge African-American rights because he is too self-absorbed with his European ideals to understand the complaints of the rioters. He in effect, does not hear the rioters as they approach him. Their demonstration makes him

> almost forget his Jaguar and Lake Bluff;
> almost forget Grandtully (which is The
> Best Thing That Ever Happened to Scotch); almost
> forgot the sculpture at the Richard Gray
> and Distelheim; the kidney pie at Maxim's,
> the Grenadine de Beouf at Maison Henri.

These items are aspects of his life in Europe that the participants in the demonstration he is witnessing oppose. Cabot and his actions are representative of the entire oppressive community.

The next line of the poem acts as a switch between Cabot's thoughts of himself to how he views the "Negroes" as they approach him. The group approaches him "…in rough ranks. / In seas. In windsweep." He is horrified with their appearance calling them "sweaty and unpretty." He is disgusted shouting "Que tu es grossier!" (How gross you are!) as though the mere presence of this group is an affront to his sensibilities. He cringes away from the crowd fearing that just being touched by the crowd will taint his pure "nourished white" self. The crowd consumes him as "It" touches and breathes on him. All the while the crowd chanting at him, mocking him, and eventually killing him as he cries out " Lord! Forgive these nigguhs that know not what they do." The obvious religious overtone of this last line refers to Jesus' dying words upon the cross, asking God to forgive his killers for their actions. The violence of the crowd in the poem is a reference to the desperate feelings that many African American activists felt after the assassination of Martin Luther King Jr. in 1968. His peaceful protests against racism while successful had a high price, and after his death many activists began looking for more direct and sometimes violent protests.

Brooks reinforces this call for action in "The Third Sermon on the Warpland" with the reference to the mythological creature, the Phoenix. The metaphor of the creature destroying itself by fire and then rising from the ashes is representative of the marchers acting out and possibly destroying themselves with the hope that they will rise up after the demonstration having achieved their goal.

Brooks uses the word sermon in the title of this poem to reaffirm the religious devotion of the civil rights activists. The use of the word Warpland refers to the current state of political and social turmoil in the United States.

Brooks begins the poem affirming the beauty of the earth. It is tranquil and pleasant. Regardless of this beauty there is still unrest. She introduces the Black philosopher who indirectly refers back to King's definition of a riot as "…the language of the unheard," stating that their oppression is like being in shackles. The "keepers" of the chains are distracted by their complacent lives, choosing to ignore the rattling of the chains. The philosopher directly addresses the audience explaining that "you don't hear the remarkable music." If the audience did hear the music, then they too would join their fight and make "The blackblues."

The tone of the poem changes in the next several stanzas as Brooks describes the riot in progress. She describes an empty restaurant, Jessie's Kitchen, where "Crazy flowers" or flames spread across the sky announcing the beginning of the riot, "hissing This is/ it."

The next stanza describes men running about, passing over albums by Bing Crosby to steal Melvin Van Peebles albums. Their choice here distinguishes them from a mindless mob to a group who even in their thievery are making a statement about their hatred for anything representing the status quo.

Brooks describes the scene further as "little rioters" steal a radio from hell (possibly a burning store) and sit down to enjoy some music from James Brown, Mingus, Young-Holt, Coleman, John. During all the chaos, they stop to enjoy the few moments when the chains do not restrict their movement. They are free, and they bond with the performers singing the blues, but it is not permanent and Brooks notes the progression with the melodic phrase, "However, what/ is going on/ is going on."

In the next stanza, Brooks uses the image of fire as a symbol of regeneration, change and hope, and quotes a White philosopher as support for the rioters actions, stating "It is better to light one candle than curse the darkness." The riot is the candle and it has been lit, but in an ironic twist, the candle does not signify improvement as the white philosopher suggests; its illumination acts as notification to the authorities that something is happening. Brooks announces the arrival of the police with the line "GUARD HERE, GUNS LOADED." Everything changes now, and Brooks describes the panic of the rioters as they run from the Law scattering through the streets.

Some of the rioters do not escape, and in the next stanza Brooks describes the death of a woman at the hands of the law. A young rioter, Yancey, makes a fleeting reference to Hemingway's novel praising bullfighting, *Death in the Afternoon,* and screams out a cheer of encouragement for the bull to kill the bullfighter. The riot is over and Brooks uses a headline from the Sun-Times to begin the next stanza.

The headline reads "Nine Die" and Brooks includes the apparent side note on the paper giving a number for concerned citizens to call and check so to curtail the rampant rumors that ran through Chicago after the riot.

The next page of the poem is a eulogy for Richard "Peanut" Washington who was the well-known and respected gang leader of the Chicago gang, the Blackstone Rangers. He is described as one who will bring about change "signature," one who is almost a religious figure "A Herald," and one who will unite the past with the present "A Span." Because he is so respected and revered he will not let his gang members get out of control. All of the other gang leaders have the same respect from their members and all the leaders decide collectively that the riot or "Passion"… "AIN'T all upinheah." or hip.

The next stanza is a statement from the white majority who cannot see their own complicity in the unfair treatment of African Americans, and they don't understand why "these people" support and participate in a riot. The only thing they see is the destruction of property. They are unable to see or hear the statement behind the riot.

Brooks ends this poem with a statement of hope reaffirming that the Phoenix, regardless of the lies and legends that are being made, will rise from the ashes.

The final section of the poem "An Aspect of Love, Alive in the Ice and Fire" is a description of the moments shared between two people after the riot. Many critics have interpreted the two people to be lovers who are enjoying time with each other. This poem can also be interpreted as a description of one moment during the riot when two people share an intimate moment with one another. The line "A physical light is in the room" is the initial spark of the phoenix igniting itself. The narrator describes the phoenix rising as "self-accepting as a lion in Afrikan velvet." The moment the narrator shares with the rising Phoenix is precious and is "the time of not-to-end." Through their participation in the riot, both of the characters in this section, the lovers, have transformed themselves into new beings. As they walk away from one another, they know that they have only just begun on their journey down the "imperturbable street." Brooks describes the street as imperturbable because it is a moment during the riot before the Law arrive and the physical violence begins.

The power of the tripart poem is in the metaphors and the images created by Brooks. The most important theme from this poem is Brooks's disciplined approach to describing the philosophy behind riots, and how riots are an instrument of change for the unheard and oppressed people.

CRITICAL VIEWS ON

"Riot"

WILLIAM H. HANSELL ON VIOLENCE IN THE SECOND PART
OF "RIOT"

[William H. Hansell is a scholar and critic who has been
published in *Black American Literature Forum, Phylon: The
Atlanta University Review of Race and Culture, Obsidian:
Black Literature in Review, Concerning Poetry and College
Language Association Journal.* In this selection, Hansell
discusses violence is subjective and what one audience may
think of as violent another may see as a demonstration or
statement and not destructive. He argues that Brooks's
poem is not about violence but about making a statement.]

The second or middle part of *Riot* is entitled "The Third Sermon on
the Warpland" (11-20). Somewhat like "In the Mecca," the narrative
perspective in this poem shifts rapidly from place to place with little
or no transition, presenting a series of scenes and speeches woven
together to present an impressionistic and deliberately fragmented
account of a ghetto riot.

Before looking at the poem a word on the title and an image
prominent in it is necessary. *Warp* derives from the Greek word
meaning to whirl, and the sermon indeed declares that a turbulent
time confronts black people. Furthermore, *warp* is often used to
describe the condition of being bent or swollen: and as an image of
distortion this is probably intended to figuratively reenforce both the
psychological warping of blacks and the socially warped forms of
living imposed upon them. There is yet another possible influence
on Brooks's choice of words. W.E.B. Du Bois wrote, "We have
woven ourselves with the very warp of this nation"; and the warp, of
course, is considered the foundation or supporting thread in weav-
ing. Read this way Brooks's metaphor suggests that blacks have
been essential to the United States even though forced to live a
warped existence and denied credit for their contributions, just as
Lucius Brockway is in *Invisible Man*. Lucius, it will be remembered,

is indispensable to the production of the "right white" paint, even though no one is able to precisely analyze what he does, and he won't tell because he believes, probably correctly, that the managers would speedily discard him if they could do without him.

A thematic carry-over from "Riot," the title poem, to "The Third Sermon" is made evident in the epigraph, which expresses the constructive and creative aspects of apparent destruction, or perhaps more precisely, the necessity of destruction to creation:

> Phoenix: "In Egyptian Mythology, a bird which lived for five hundred years and then consumed itself in fire, rising renewed from the ashes."
> —Webster.

Destruction producing rebirth is a major theme in the poem. Nonetheless, the opening lines of the poem mark a sharp contrast to the epigraph.

> The earth is a beautiful place.
> Watermirrors and things to be reflected.
> Goldenrod across the little lagoon.

Following this is a statement by "the Black Philosopher," a statement which attempts to explain why blacks are now convinced that violence is essential. First, however, it is important to analyze the function of the three opening lines.

The introduction stresses the earth's beauty, but it also emphasizes a perspective: the beauty is "reflected" and it is "across the little lagoon." Although there is the affirmative note, there is also the revelation that awareness of beauty, however humanizing, is not the same as participation.

With the Black Philosopher's words the social and personal implications of the opening ideas are made more definite:

> "Our chains are in the keep of the keeper
> in a labeled cabinet
> on the second shelf by the cookies . . .
> sonatas. the arabesques . . .
> There's a rattle, sometimes.
> You do not hear it who mind only
> cookies and crunch them.
> You do not hear the remarkable music—'A

Death Song For You Before You Die.'
If You could hear it
you would make music too.
The *black*blues."

The importance of black people determining their identity, of wrest-
ing "the Negro image from white control" rather than submitting to
traditional stereotypes or merely becoming white men in dark-face,
has of course been pointed out by numerous writers. Brooks's
kitchen-item metaphor, in fact, might be a specific allusion to
Melvin B. Tolson's answer to the question "Who is a Negro?": "The
Negro is a dish in the white man's kitchen—a potpourri . . . ." So it
is that the Black Philosopher declares that blacks must take something back in order to be free of their "chains." Along with reminders
of slavery, exploitation, and violent suppression, we are told that
they are kept "on the second shelf by the cookies . . . ," suggesting,
I believe that "the keeper" (white society *and* black acquiescence?)
has grown so used to this possession, power, or powerlessness, that
"he" takes it entirely for granted. The attitude echoes the idea stated
in the epigraph to the entire collection—the Negro will be our friend
no matter what we do to him.

The philosopher is aware that the occasional "rattle" has been
ignored, which is to say in America every indication of dissatisfac-
tion with the status of blacks has been relatively ignored. "The
Keeper" concerns himself with crunching "cookies," with anything
at all, perhaps. So the "remarkable music" announcing the death of
such attitudes has, until now, gone unheard. To the extent blacks in
the past did resist their "chains," she says, they cooperated with and
strengthened their "Keeper." Now, as the Philosopher declares, that
time is over. The old relationships, whether all blacks and whites are
aware of it or not, are being shattered.

After the Philosopher's speech—the first of three—there follow
seven lines portraying a cafe or restaurant where no one is eating
because the customers have gone to participate in the riot or are star-
ing in rapt attention at the smile and flames billowing over rooftops.
Normal activities are suspended:

> nobody's eating Jessie's Perfect Food.
> Crazy flowers
> cry up across the sky, spreading and hissing
> *This is it.*

The young blacks run to join in the riot. With the description of their eagerness to participate, Brooks portrays concretely an instance of the Black Philosopher's earlier generalizations. These young people have some sense of retrieving things which belong to them:

> The Young men run.
> They will not steal Bing Crosby but will steal
> Melvin Van Peebles who made Lillie a thing of
>   Zamphougi
> a thing of red wiggles and trebbles . . . [.]

The young men will steal the records by Peebles, an actor, writer, filmmaker, and rock-and-roll singer, because his works celebrate black pride and black awareness. The rioters also steal recordings by black musicians: "Mingus, Young-Holt, Coleman, John . . . ." In this sense, it is not a typical riot; it is not a "clean riot." That is to say, the intention of the children is not simply to steal a few records. At this point, however, the narrator seems to despair of explaining to white people the difference between the riot in progress and ordinary riots, and interrupts the narrative with lines which seem to express the impossibility of every explaining what the riot means:

> However, what
> is going on
> is going on.

But the narrator has not actually given up the attempt to explain the behavior of the rioters. Drawing back from the immediate scene, the narrator literally states that the destruction going on will provide the means to a clearer vision:

> Fire,
> That is there way of lighting candles in the dark-
>   ness.
> A white Philosopher said
> 'It is better to light one candle than curse the
>   darkness.'
>   These candles curse—
> inverting the deeps of the darkness.

The seeming paradox of increasing darkness by "lighting candles" expresses, perhaps, the essence of the Black Mystique. Darkness, blackness, is their identity and being; therefore, to destroy every-thing that distorts or inhibits their darkness is to gain the truth about themselves and the freedom to be themselves. It is ironic, of course, that the "white Philosopher's" nostrum has to be reversed in order to have positive significance for the black man. Candles are lit to increase darkness; destruction becomes creation.

The Book of Amos in the Old Testament may have been one influence on Brooks in her choice of darkness as a metaphor for cataclysmic change:

> the day of the Lord is darkness
>
> . . .
>
> Shall not the day of the Lord be
> darkness and not light? even very dark,
> and so brightness in it? (5:18 and 5:20)

The Lord's day of darkness will see evil punished and virtue restored.

From the candles, the narrative turns to the immediate events. The commands of police or national guardsmen are heard, the children run about, and "The Law comes sirening across the town." I believe Brooks describes the talk of the children in the streets as "ritual chatter" to reenforce the idea that at some level they are aware of the profound transformation which is occurring.

Immediately following the announcement of the law's siren, there is a passage an a woman who has been killed. It is not stated that the police or national guardsmen killed her, nor is it suggested that rioters did. There is no overt attempt to give her death or life any direct connection to the riot, its causes, or its significance. The woman is simply a victim, and all that one can certainly conclude is that life was precious to her. Her end has been ignominious, seemingly pointless, and with it Brooks may be suggesting that a black person's death, like Pepita's in "In the Mecca," has never mattered to whites.

> A woman is dead,
> Motherwoman.
> She lies among the boxes
>
> . . .
>
> That was a gut gal.

A young boys' voice follows the passage on the dead woman. From what he says it is clear that the violence and killings are not merely gestures of defiance, not merely symbolic, but spring from an outraged sense of having tolerated falseness too long, as well as from the desire to respond authentically:

> "We'll do an us!" yells Yancey, a twittering
>   twelve.
> "Instead of your deathintheafternoon,
> kill 'em, bull!
> kill 'em, bull!"

I have some difficulty accepting these words, with their reference to Hemingway, as being likely to come from the mouth of a young boy, but considered apart from the speaker, the words suggest that blacks reject violence and killing for its own sake, or for vaguely symbolic reasons, especially when the symbolism could readily be used against them. Yancey's shouted "We'll do an us!" on the other hand, suggests that violence done by blacks will have great personal, and probably racial and social significance and will not be merely symbolic. The irony here, perhaps, is that Yancey (Yankee?) voices an attitude towards violence that suggests a traditional American attitude. Violence in this tradition has been justified only as a necessary evil, a last resort when all other appeals have failed. Even chauvinistic interpretations of our national mission to carry Democracy to all people—by force if necessary—is rationalized on the ground that the violence subserves a higher end.

Following Yancey's shouts, the black Philosopher speaks for the second time. He blares:

> "I tell you, exhaustive black integrity
> would assure a blackless America . . ."

Brooks has stressed the second syllable of *exhaustive*, as if to say that when blackness is completely drawn out, completely expressed, racial conflicts will vanish. Black integrity would seem to mean, then, the condition in which black men could develop to their full potential as humans, which in turn, would mean that white men, who have been the chief obstacle to that development, would finally have recognized that what men of different races have in common is more important than differences in color. A "blackless America" would result because color differences would have no significance.

There is barely time to reflect on the Black Philosopher's words, which end in ellipsis, before the narrative shifts suddenly. The minor theme of the obtuseness of white men is again stressed. As if to underscore the unlikelihood of the Philosopher's words or the events themselves being understood, the narrator reports how the riot will be handled in a newspaper:

> Nine die, Sun-Times will tell
> and will tell too
> in small black-bordered oblongs *"Rumor? check it*
> *at 744-4111."*

The newspaper passage is followed, without transition, by a fifteen-line section entitled "A Poem to Peanut." The "Poem" describes those who are already organized against society to prey upon others. In this brief description of the response of street gang members Brooks emphasizes two things: they keep their "cool"; and they evidently see in the riot a justification of their antisocial life.

> This Peanut will not let his men explode.
> . . .
> The Disciples
> stir and thousandfold confer
> with ranging Rangermen;
> mutual in their "Yeah!—
> this AIN'T all upinheah!"

These gang members interpret the riot, in which ordinarily docile and lawabiding citizens participate, as a confirmation of their own attitudes towards society. Their sense of hostility and alienation and their attempts to be a law unto themselves seem justified by the police and guardsmen arrayed against them and by the manifestations of outrage and rebellion against authority they see all around them. Yet they are not, like the other, impelled by passions momentarily aroused. Their alienation is deeper, and they will not "explode." The gang members confer only among themselves ("thou confer / with ranging Rangermen"), implying that they will exploit the riot for their own ends. Brooks seems to suggest that unlike others involved in the riot, these gang members will not be regenerated, will not develop communal identity and interests. Their alienation has progressed too far and their only loyalty will continue to be the gang.

After the "Poem to Peanut" the narrator reports white responses to the riot.

> "But WHY do These People offend *themselves*?"
>   say they
> who say also "It's time.
> It's time to help
> These People."

Obviously, Brooks is emphasizing the urgency whites seem to understand in the abstract but cannot feel as a matter of immediate human concern. Also, the whites misinterpret the significance of the riots, concluding that the blacks are simply hurting themselves; whereas what Brooks portrays is a community, unable any longer to quietly accept deprivation, being renewed in its solidarity, its sense of identity, and taking a necessary first step. For, as the last seven lines reveal, despite white incomprehension and resistance, something of value is born out of the riots. Alluding to the epigraph, subsequent lines state something has been born:

> Lies are told and legends made.
> Phoenix rises unafraid.

The final speech of the Black Philosopher closes the poem.

> The Black Philosopher will remember:
> "There they came to life and exulted,
> the hurt mute.
> Then it was over.
> The dust, as they say, settled." (20)

The "hurt mute," black Americans, can no longer be silent or passive. The message for whites seems to be the revelation that when they acted, which wasn't often enough, self-interest and ignorance prevented any real good from occurring. Blacks now surely want no part in plans to make them like whites in so far as that means that they must be tolerant of prejudice, and indifferent—or accommodating to injustice and deprivation.

—William H. Hansell, "The Role of Violence in Recent Poems of Gwendolyn Brooks." *Studies in Black Literature* 5 (1974): pp. 22-25.

Norris B. Clark on Brooks' Themes of Love in Her Later Works

[Norris B. Clark is the director of Black Studies and associate professor of English at Bradley University. He is a well-published essayist and commentator on the work of Gwendolyn Brooks, Amiri Baraka, Michael S. Harper, and Toni Morrison. In this selection Clark discusses Brooks' attitude toward racists in her poetry and her life, and he demonstrates that her late poetry is a reflection of her compassion and love for humanity.]

In essence, Gwendolyn Brooks's thematic concerns, the tense and complex dimensions of living through the paths of petty destinies, have changed but have not eliminated an acceptance of those who choose to live and to love differently. Unlike the more radical black aesthetic poets, she does not condemn the "Intellectual Audience" as Nikki Giovanni has done, or equate Negroes with repulsive beasts as does Welton Smith in "The Nigga Section," or curse white people, as in Carolyn Rodgers's "The Last M. F." Brooks's later works, *Riot*, *Aloneness*, *Family Pictures*, and *Beckonings*, instead, emphasize a need for black unity by using "the exile rhythms of a Black people still seeking to establish at-homeness in America," but not to the exclusion of universal themes and subjects such as "brotherly love," literary critics, heroes, music, love between man and woman, false ideals, friendship, beautiful black blues. Nor like the more radical or political black poets of the sixties and early seventies such as Imamu Baraka, Sonia Sanchez, the "radical" phase of Nikki Giovanni, Welton Smith, or other black aesthetic advocates does Brooks create racist, propagandistic, and taciturn poems that advocate violence as therapeutic (Fanon's dictum), exhort whites to bring about equality, castigate or demean others. Instead, she depicts black realities without brutally frank language via her black voice, a voice that emanates a conscious humanistic concern for others. Similar to "great masters," Brooks's poetry does not tell us that there is evil, corruption, oppression, futility, or racism; rather, she shows us the tragedy and its relationship to individuals in hopes that we may learn a moral insight from the juxtaposition of beauty and horror, death in life as in "The Life of Lincoln West."

Brooks's unique voice in her latest poetry is one that not only ide-ologically varies from a narrowly defined black aesthetic, but also thematically deviates from its total reliance on obscure African ref-erences or Africa as a source of inspiration or upon a doctrine of how to live, as in Ron Karenga's Kawaida Doctrine, or a pro-Muslim reli-gious orientation as some black aestheticians advocate:

> Blackness
> is a going to essences and to unifyings.
> "MY NAME IS AFRIKA!"
> Well, every fella's a Foreign Country.
> This Foreign Country speaks to you.
> (FP, 15)

Not surprisingly, Brooks's voice which contrasts the American ideals and practices—W. E. B. Du Bois's "Veil Metaphor"—espe-cially the insensitivity and ignorance of whites toward blacks, as in *Riot*, is not filled with private symbolism or biting satire. Rather, self-identity in Brooks's poems leads to group-identity. She does not, as Baraka has done, only focus on a black nationalist, black Muslim, black power, or blacker-than-black perspective. Rather, her voice is one that recreates the feelings and thoughts of the unheard, as riots do, rather than merely languish in a black aesthetic of polemics devoid of lyricism. Even though Brooks's poetry calls for a black dignity and a black pride, erstwhile symbolized by Africa, she acknowledges that blacks "know so little of that long leap lan-guid land [Africa]" and suggests that enacting "our inward law"—unity (community, family) among black Americans—is more impor-tant than any external reliances upon a leader, a god or God(s) or the heat of "easy griefs that fool and fuel nothing" (*Beckonings*, 15–16). Her attempt to create black unity is not to establish a bond among third-world peoples but to establish a bond between those oppressed black Americans who are defining their own Roof. . . ." Consequently, her content is not only specifically American but is, more so than many writers of a black aesthetic persuasion, also reflective of the attitudes, aspirations, and concerns of black Americans as they historically have been confronted with the denial of American ideals, racism, and pathos of human choice.

Unlike the black writers of polemics and propaganda or the rhetoricians of hate and violence, Brooks doesn't attempt to impose her personal philosophy upon others; she does not demean or denigrate blacks whose psychological mechanism to survive leads them to be "Toms" or race traitors. (In fact, some critics have questioned her attitudes or personal voice as not being strong enough on issues such as abortion.) Brooks's poetry remains one of love and affirmation, one that accepts some hate and perhaps some violence as necessary without condemning or castigating those who have been pawns to interracial and intraracial forces. Adequately reflecting the hopes and aspirations of the black community, Brooks displays a love for her brothers and sisters regardless of psychosocial or socioeconomic position. In doing so, she clearly embraces "blackness" and the values of liberation, and thus the values of all humanity. That quality, despite an emphasis on embracing blacks first, is one that is universal in literature of self-affirmation and self-identity; the universal is revealed through the particular. As her sensitivity to the spirit of social revolution emanates from her sense of "love," Brooks advocates a sense of self-love and compassion while reflecting the tensions of her time period, a tension due to racial oppression: "On the street we smile./We go/in different directions/down the imperturbable street" (*Riot*, 22).

—Norris B. Clark, "Gwendolyn Brooks and the Black Aesthetic."*A Life Distilled: Gwendolyn Brooks, Her Poetry and Fiction.* eds. Maria K. Mootry and Gary Smith (Urbana, IL: University of Illinois Press, 1987): pp. 90-92.

D. H. MELHEM ON JOHN CABOT IN THE POEM

[This extract by Melhem describes a few of the explanations and interpretation about the use of the historical figure John Cabot in the poem.]

Intricate, richly allusive, "Riot" lattices imagery and concepts through its central figure, John Cabot, archetypal bigot and snob. His typology and tastes (Jaguar, art objects, the best food and liquor) strategically mirror his own stereotyping. "John Cabot, out of Wilma, once a Wycliffe, / all whitebluerose below his golden hair," categorizes him as flag-wrapped American WASP (white Anglo-Saxon Protestant), and wryly if not mischievously relates him to the author of the epigraph, Martin Luther King. John Wycliffe was an English forerunner of the Protestant Reformation, later led by Martin Luther in Germany. Although he died naturally, Wycliffe is considered a martyr because, in 1415, his body was dug up according to the wishes of Pope Martin V, and burned. John Cabot, a name synonymous from Colonial times with prominent settlers of Massachusetts, was a fifteenth-century Genoese navigator who, interestingly, bad visited Mecca. He was commissioned by Henry VII of England to find a passage to India. Thus the three Johns are linked, the contemporary one parodic of those who were brave, adventurous, and righteous. "Wycliffe" is an especially just reference, his firm anti-Church-establishment position a foil to the protagonist's ruling-class mentality. The "General Prologue" to Wycliffe's translation of the Bible (1384) reads: "This Bible is for the Government of the People, by the People, and for the People" (cf. reference to the Gettysburg Address in the Don Lee stanza of "In the Mecca").

Contrasts also implement the "failed religion" theme, already noted in "In the Mecca," opposing the bigot's corrupt Christianity to integrity of the past. Thus the first line, with fine compression, assigns the subject his unheroic attributes. The phrase "out of Wilma," moreover, suggests terminology of the stable. Brooks's only comment to me on the name "Wilma" inferred an elevated social connotation (like the Chicago suburb Wilmette), but the alternate reference is not unfamiliar to her.

The spirits of prophetic Amos and Way-out Morgan preside implacably over Cabot's portrait. Their foretold "blood bath" and "Day of Debt-pay" arrives in an apocalypse of fire, smoke, and destruction—the "fire next time" which the Lord promised Noah, in the words of the Negro spiritual. Corruption and perversion of Christianity, the "failed religion" theme—actually that of a failed humanity—appear in Cabot's vain cries to God, "Don't let It touch me! the blackness! Lord!" When it does, skepticism attaches to his "old averted doubt." At point of death, nevertheless, he calls out, "Lord! / Forgive these nigguhs that know not what they do," parodying Jesus' words upon the Cross, "Father, forgive them; for they know not what they do" (Luke, 23:24). An incidental irony (also noted by Shaw): Cabot's initials are those of Jesus Christ.

Antithesis figures largely in the imagery. Cabot's accusation "Gross. Gross. *Que tu es grossier*" ("How gross you are") which Brooks intends as his judgment of the scene and the rioters, may well be observed of Cabot himself "*Grossier*" derives from the French *gros*, meaning corpulent or coarse. Coupled with the "nourished white" of his skin and/or attire, "gross" emphasizes the rich food and rich life Cabot has enjoyed ("the kidney pie at Maxim's, / the Grenadine de Boeuf at Maison Henri"). The impoverished blacks symbolically confront these luxurious images with "pig foot, chitterling, and cheap chili," mounting their ruggedly simple food against his spiritual coarseness. In one sense, opposition levels both classes; in another, it reverses them. There is crudity even in Cabot's appeal "to any handy angel in the sky." Of course the plea to God is raised in extremis, and the poet's sarcasm leans heavily.

Triadic structures permeate the imagery—Cabot/Wilma/Wycliffe; whitebluerose; pig foot/chitterling/cheap chili—and recur. Heavy alliteration weights the hauteur, the posturing of Cabot images and their touch of French affectation. Cabot is anything but heroic; the stylistic device obliquely prefigures the perverse heroic of the mob. Yet the dominantly iambic pentameter announces blank verse, potentially a heroic meter. Despite random and slant rhyme, however, it suggests the conventional quality of Cabot and ironically presses him to a typological grid. Brooks uses capitalization for satiric emphasis; "Grandtully (which is The Best Thing That Ever Happened to Scotch)" suggests an advertising slogan. Cabot's portrait emerges: received ideas, tastes, beliefs, snobbery and prejudice, the vulgar pastiche of a class.

As victim and murderers converge, cause and effect blur into broken glass, smoke, and fire. Beyond God's apocalyptic ire lies the subject: blood-guilt, its origin, consequences, and cure. Cabot retains his blasphemous assumption of primacy as Son of God. His last words, parodic of Jesus, signal a lack of insight or humility and touch his final outcry with grisly humor.

The rioters, frenzied and blindly raging, resemble agents of the Furies. "Riot" introduces the matter of blood-guilt in a clear, spare manner, analogous to that of Aeschylus in his trilogy *The Oresteia*, which studies the curse on the House of Atreus. In Aeschylus, the idea, religious or moral, coheres; in Brooks, typology serves. Both writers implicitly ask, "How, by what shall I live?" and answer.

—D. H. Melhem, "Riot, Family Pictures, Aloneness." *Gwendolyn Brooks: Poetry and the Heroic Voice*. (Lexington, Kentucky: The University Press of Kentucky, 1987): pp. 193-195.

CHARLES L. JAMES ON BROOKS' TRANSITION FROM HER EARLIER POETRY

[Charles L. James is a critic and scholar who has been published in *Studies in Black Literature, Obsidian: Black Literature in Review, The Langston Hughes Review.* In this selection James discusses some of the factors that Brooks describes as the turning point in her poetic voice.]

In what has since become a well-known episode, Gwendolyn Brooks describes an auspicious turning point in her career, a turning point that came in 1967 when she attended the Second Black Writers' Conference at Fisk University in Nashville. The Pulitzer prize-winning poet was stunned and intrigued by the energy and electricity generated by LeRoi Jones (Amiri Baraka) and Ron Milner, among others, on that predominantly black campus. The excitement was at once surprising, stirring, and contagious, and Brooks admits that from that moment she entered a "new consciousness." She had discovered a "new" audience: young people full of a fresh spirit and ready, as she characterized them, to take on the challenges. The sturdy ideas that she earlier held were no longer valid in this "new world," and several years later she would untendentiously remark: "I am trying to weave the coat that I shall wear."

The older coat that Brooks doffed is made of the material for which she is best known: such vignettes of ghetto people in Chicago as "The Anniad," "The Sundays of Satin-Legs Smith," "The Bean Eaters," or "We Real Cool," for example. They are works of a poet who brings a patrician mind to a plebeian language; a poet always searching for the stirring, unusual coloration of words; the poet in whom Addison Gayle, Jr., has noted what he calls "a tendency toward obscurity and abstraction" and "a child-like fascination for words." But, like Emily Dickinson, Brooks searched for fresh sounds and imagery produced by word clusters that startle rather than obscure:

> Let it be stairways, and a splintery box
> Where you have thrown me, scraped me with your kiss,
> Have honed me, have released me after this
> Cavern Kindness, smiled away our shocks.

Most of her poems written before 1967—before the Fisk conferences—are her "front yard songs," poems that reflect the self-consciousness of a poet whose audience seeks lessons in a lyric that ostensibly transcends race. They are solid, highly imaginative poems, and if they suggest comparisons with Wallace Stevens, as several critics have noted, they also recall Emily Dickinson's ingenuity with language, her ironic ambiguities:

> A light and diplomatic bird
> Is lenient in my window tree.
> A quick dilemma of the leaves
> Discloses twist and tact to me.

They recall as well the "grotesques" who habituate the fictional world of Sherwood Anderson's Winesburg, Ohio:

> True, there is silver under
> The veils of the darkness,
> But few care to dig in the night
> For the possible treasure of stars.

But above all, there is the unmistakable rhythmic shifting—"My hand is stuffed with mode, design, device./But I lack access to my proper stone"—and the haunting incongruity—"Believe that ever in my deliberateness I was not deliberate."

The startling Fisk conference may be viewed metaphorically as Brooks's peek at "the back yard" ("Where it's rough and untended and hungry weed grows")—the escape, as George Kent says, from the highly ordered and somewhat devitalized life of her "front yard training." The backyard offers a new vitality, a new consciousness. Brooks, around fifty years old at the time of the conference, strikes up a dialogue in free verse with the subjects of her earlier poetry. The distances narrow and the angles flatten: "we are each other's/harvest:/we are each other's business:/we are each other's magnitude and bond."

The angles of vision have changed to suit what Brooks describes as "my newish voice": "[It] will not be an imitation of the contemporary young black voice, which I so admire, but an extending adaptation of today's G.B. [sic] voice." So there is something of a near elegiac tone in Brooks's "transcendence" of her poetic past; but it is elegy without regrets, for she has moved from a place of "knowledgeable unknowing" to a place of "Know-now" preachments.

> I tell you
> I love You
> and I trust You.
> Take my Faith.
> Make of my Faith an engine.
> Make of my Faith
> a Black Star. I am Beckoning.

—Charles L. James, " Gwendolyn Brooks: Overview." *Contemporary Poets* 6th ed. Thomas Riggs (New York: St. James Press, 1996). pp. 116-117.

"Queen of the Blues"

This poem is found in the collection of poems called *A Street in Bronzeville* (1945). The poems in this collection mark the beginning of Brooks' career as a poet; furthermore, these poems establish certain themes that will grow with Brooks's career: family, gender inequality, racism and social equality. Although Brooks will not become personally and actively involved in Black Activist groups until 1967, many of the poems in *A Street in Bronzeville* (1945) introduce some of these themes.

The poem "Queen of the Blues" details many of the ideas Brooks has about the treatment women and their position in society. Her treatment of the strong black woman who must overcome sexist and racist attacks is evident in this poem, but she also demonstrates the strong emotional mindset that a woman must have in order to overcome the oppressive tendencies in society.

The title of the poem introduces the audience to two important concepts: queen and blues. There is the obvious reference to nobility in the use of queen; however, given the connection between the use of the name Mame to popular blues singers of the past like Bessie Smith, Ma' Rainey, and Billie Holiday, the use of queen is more closely associated to some hierarchy in the blues.

From the beginning of the poem, Brooks sets the tone by using the name "Mame." This could possibly be a symbolic reference to her own mother who we learn later in the poem has died a few years back. She will now be her own mother.

The words chosen by Brooks reveal Mame's social status. Within the first four lines of the poem a great deal is revealed about Mame. The fact that she is a singer at a venue called the Midnight Club and that "the place was red/ With blues" suggests a less than ideal environment. In the 1940's being a singer in and of itself may not have been a bad profession; however, when that profession is coupled with the next few images, Midnight Club and red, the profession begins to lose its stature. At the time, singing in a club that is open that late was not a sign that the club was of a high repute. The use of the word "red" is also very suggestive. On the one hand, the physical location may have a red hue in the air due to poor lighting and stage lighting in the club. On the other hand the color may be describing the location of the club in the red light district of Chicago. Any interpretation of red is going to be tainted because it is followed by the prepositional phrase "With Blues." Red with blues, the blues are saturated by the red environment; there is no escape. The only relief is through expression. Her chosen form of expression is singing the blues.

Mame's only release is singing and shaking ". . . her body/ Across the floor." Now the scene is set for Brooks to switch from the physical description of the club and Mame to the status of Mame's emotional state. Through an omniscient third person narrator, possibly a person sitting in the audience listening to the show, the reader learns about Mame's life and internal struggles. The internal exploration begins with the line "For what did she have/ To lose?" The narrator now begins to justify Mame's choice to perform in this club. What does Mame have to lose? The narrator does not assume that Mame would lose anything tangible or even that Mame's internal feelings or emotions would be lost but rather that her only motivation for not singing in the club would be to maintain the respect of important people in her life. Each one of the next seven stanzas represent the respect of people in her life that she would not want to lose by singing in this club and shaking her body across the floor.

In the second stanza, the narrator explains that Mame's mother is dead, indicating that she would not lose the respect of her mother because her mother has already been taken from her. The narrator pities Mame because she does not have a "Legal Pa/ To Shame/ Her off the floor/ Of the Midnight Club." Mame does not have an older brother as a protector or a younger brother for whom she should be a role model. She doesn't have a "baby girl [Daughter]" or a "Sonny Boy" [son] to inspire her to maintain her morality. It is as if the narrator is actually trying to convince Mame that she has nothing to lose, and in the next stanza Mame begins to convince herself in her own voice, complete with the repetition so prevalent in blues lyrics, "Show me a man/What will love me Till I die./ Now show me a man/ What will love me/ Till I die'" Mame is adding to the list, stating that she does not have a husband/ lover/ boyfriend to stop her from performing. Furthermore, Mame elaborates her isolated state through a brief narrative about her "daddy" a reference to a boyfriend, "sugar daddy," or a man she thought could fill the void left by her lost father. The interpretation of "daddy" is not as important as the result of the relationship. She works hard; he spends her money; he leaves her for another woman who is "… gonna be/ Black and blue" after Mame gets through with her.

At this point, when Mame is close to confirming that she does not have anything to lose by performing, the M.C. of the club glorifies her as "Queen of the blues" and she likes it—she snaps her fingers and rolls her hips at the attention the title gives to her. The question is repeated "What did she have/ To lose?" Mame begins to question the validity of the title, Queen, stating "Men don't tip their/ Hats to me./ They pinch my arms/ And they slap my thighs./ But when has a man/Tipped his hat to me?" The power in this simple question lies within Mame who recognizes the term Queen as a title demanding respect. Brooks demonstrates the power of this conclusion not only through the use of exclamation marks but also altering the metre and form of the poem from eight line stanzas to two quatrains.

There is a progression throughout the poem. By the end of the poem Mame has answered the question. The only thing that she has to lose now is the respect she has for herself. The final two lines of the poem reiterate this realization as Mame accepts the title queen. It is unclear whether Mame decides to continue singing at the club or not but the important point that Brooks is making is that she alone, as an independent African-American woman, will chose what is best for her. She does not need to act morally for her mother, father, older brother, younger brother, daughter, son, husband, lover, the M.C.; she only needs to be true to herself.

"Queen of the Blues"

GARY SMITH ON THE HARLEM RENAISSANCE IN THE POEM

[In this extract, Smith discusses the powerful image of Black women in Brooks's poetry.]

In this short, introductory poem Brooks, in a manner reminiscent of Eliot's alienated Waste Land characters, looks not toward a glorified African past or limitless future, but rather at a stifled present. Her old lovers ponder not an image of their racial past or some symbolized possibility of self-renewal, but rather the overwhelming question of what to do in the here-and-now. Moreover, their world, circumscribed by the incantatory line that opens and closes the poem, But in the crowding darkness not a word did they say, is one that is distinctly at odds with their lives. They move timidly through the crowded darkness of their neighborhood largely ignorant of the season, May, the lateness of the hour, midnight, and a particular raison d'etre, a time for loving. Their attention, we infer, centers upon the implicit need to escape any peril that might consume what remains of their lives. The tempered optimism in the poem, as the title indicates, is the fact that they are old-marrieds: a social designation that suggests the longevity of their lives and the solidity of their marital bond in what is, otherwise, an ephemeral world of change. Indeed, as the prefatory poem in A Street in Bronzeville, the old marrieds, on the whole debunks one of the prevalent motifs of Harlem Renaissance poetry: its general optimism about the future.

As much as the Harlem Renaissance was noted for its optimism, an important corollary motif was that of ethnic or racial pride. This pride—often thought a reaction to the minstrel stereotypes in the Dunbar tradition—usually focused with romantic idealization upon the Black woman. . . .

In A Street in Bronzeville, this romantic impulse for idealizing the Black woman runs headlong into the biting ironies of intraracial discrimination. In poem after poem in A Street in Bronzeville, within the well-observed caste lines of skin color, the consequences of dark pigmentation are revealed in drastic terms. One of the more popular of these poems, The Ballad of Chocolate Mabbie, explores the tragic ordeal of Mabbie, the Black female heroine, who is victimized by her dark skin and her saucily bold lover, Willie Boone.... Mabbie's life, of course, is one of unrelieved monotony; her social contacts are limited to those who, like her, are dark skinned, rather than lemon-hued or light skinned. But as Brooks makes clear, the larger tragedy of Mabbie's life is the human potential that is squandered:

> Oh, warm is the waiting for joys, my dears! And it cannot be
> too long. O, pity the little poor Chocolate lips
> That carry the bubble of song!

But if Mabbie is Brooks's parodic victim of romantic love, her counterpart in Ballad of Pearl May Lee realizes a measure of sweet revenge. In outline, Brooks's poem is reminiscent of Cullen's The Ballad of the Brown Girl (1927). There are, however, several important differences. The first is the poem's narrative structure: Pearl May Lee is betrayed in her love for a Black man who couldn't abide dark meat, who subsequently makes love to a white girl and is lynched for his crime of passion, whereas Cullen's Brown Girl is betrayed in her love for a white man, Lord Thomas, who violated explicit social taboo by marrying her rather than Fair London, a white girl. Moreover, Cullen's poem, a ballad retold, is traditional in its approach to the ballad form. . . . Brooks's ballad, on the other hand, dispenses with the rhetorical invocation of the traditional ballad and begins in medias res:

> Then off they took you, off to the jail,
> A hundred hooting after.
> And you should have heard me at my house.
> I cut my lungs with my laughter,
> Laughter, Laughter.
> I cut my lungs with my laughter.

This mocking tone is sustained throughout the poem, even as Sammy, Pearl May Lee's lover, is lynched:

> You paid for your dinner, Sammy boy,
> And you didn't pay with money.
> You paid with your hide and my heart, Sammy boy,

For your taste of pink and white honey,
Honey, Honey,
For your taste of pink and white honey.

Here, one possible motif in the poem is the price that Pearl May
Lee pays for her measure of sweet revenge: the diminution of her
own capacity to express love and compassion for another—however
ill-fated—human being. But the element of realism that Brooks
injects into her ballad by showing Pearl May Lee's mocking detachment from her lover's fate is a conscious effort to devalue the romantic idealization of Black love. Furthermore, Pearl May Lee's
macabre humor undermines the racial pride and harmony that was
an important tenet in the Renaissance prescription for the New
Negro. And, lastly, Pearl May Lee's predicament belies the social
myth of the Black woman as objective correlative of the
Renaissance's romanticism. . . .

For Brooks, unlike the Renaissance poets, the victimization of
poor Black women becomes not simply a minor chord but a predominant theme of A Street in Bronzeville. Few, if any, of her female
characters are able to free themselves from the web of poverty and
racism that threatens to strangle their lives. The Black heroine in
obituary for a living lady was decently wild / As a child, but as a victim of society's hypocritical, puritan standards, she fell in love with
a man who didn't know / That even if she wouldn't let him touch her
breasts she / was still worth his hours. In another example of the
complex life-choices confronting Brooks's women, the two sisters
of Sadie and Maude must choose between death-in-life and life-in-
death. Maude, who went to college, becomes a thin brown mouse,
presumably resigned to spinsterhood, living all alone / In this old
house, while Sadie who scraped life / With a fine-tooth comb bears
two illegitimate children and dies, leaving as a heritage for her children her fine-tooth comb. What is noticeable in the lives of these
Black women is a mutual identity that is inextricably linked with
race and poverty. . . .

Brooks's relationship with the Harlem Renaissance poets, as A
Street in Bronzeville ably demonstrates, was hardly imitative. As
one of the important links with the Black poetic tradition of the
1920s and 1930s, she enlarged the element of realism that was an
important part of the Renaissance world-view. Although her poetry

is often conditioned by the optimism that was also a legacy of the period, Brooks rejects outright their romantic prescriptions for the lives of Black women. And in this regard, she serves as a vital link with the Black Arts Movement of the 1960s that, while it witnessed the flowering of Black women as poets and social activists as well as the rise of Black feminist aesthetics in the 1970s, brought about a curious revival of romanticism in the Renaissance mode.

However, since the publication of A Street in Bronzeville, Brooks has not eschewed the traditional roles and values of Black women in American society; on the contrary, in her subsequent works, Annie Allen (1949), The Bean Eaters (1960), and The Mecca (1968), she has been remarkably consistent in identifying the root cause of intraracial problems within the Black community as white racism and its pervasive socio-economic effects. Furthermore, as one of the chief voices of the Black Arts Movement, she has developed a social vision, in such works as Riot (1969), Family Pictures (1970), and Beckonings (1975), that describes Black women and men's equally integral parts of the struggle for social and economic justice....

—Gary Smith, "Gwendolyn Brooks's 'A Street in Bronzeville', the Harlem Renaissance and the Mythologies of Black Women." *MELUS* 10, no. 3 (1983): pp. 33-46.

D. H. MELHEM ON THE QUEEN'S THEMES

[This extract by Melhem is a brief description of the major themes in the poem and how they can be interpreted.]

While "Queen of the Blues" shows the influence of Langston Hughes in style and subject, it remains technically unique. Brooks employs both a recast ballad form and the blues proper, the former in third person, the latter in the woman's confessional song. Speech and music commingle. The ballad/blues confluence displays Brooks at her best "Tuned Ear," at ease with Southern black musical and linguistic elements. The blues itself is the musical genre developed out of Negro work songs, hollers, and spirituals, popularized through the vocal style of W. C. Handy around 1912 (Major, 29). Its lyrics involve repetition at the beginning of each passage, with a rhyming conclusion. Poets, in modifying the traditional three-line, twelve-bar pattern, have expanded the variations which appear to some extent in music. Brooks's twelve stanzas suggest the twelve bars of the form.

> Mame was singing
> At the Midnight Club.
> And the place was red
> With blues.
> She could shake her body
> Across the floor.
> For what did she have
> to lose?

The closing couplet (repetend) establishes the narrator's presence.

The first five stanzas of the ninety-two lines describe the Queen's background, her unknown father, her love for her mother, whom she mourned "with roses and tears," her lack of a family life, her essential solitude. These facts lend context and continuity to the blues soliloquy that follows. The Queen sings the loneliness of her life, how she loved a man who left her for another woman after she worked as a domestic for whites, "Scrubbed hard" in their kitchens, and gave him her earnings. As "daddy" he connotes her disappointing father.

After the M.C.'s introduction, Mame reflects on her wounded majesty. Why don't men tip their hats to her? Stanza 11 functions as chorus, a ragtime-sounding, huckstering quatrain, repeating the M.C.'s public appraisal, "Strictly, strictly, / The queen of the blues!" In stanza 12, however, the M.C.'s voice merges with the woman's private, closing lament and develops an ambiguous yet dramatic identity into choral comment, as in classical Greek plays.

Mame/narrator/chorus concludes that "Men are low down / Dirty and mean." John T. Shawcross reminds that "low down and dirty" is a frequent epitome in jazz lyrics and card playing. He suspects that in the background is a blues called "Jelly, Jelly," written by Earl "Fatha" Hines and Billy Eckstine, and well known as performed by Hines and Josh White. In the song, "jellyroll," which has sexual connotations, has killed the narrator's mother and blinded his father, and the human condition is referred to as "low down and dirty."

The Queen feels empty and abandoned. Respectability eludes her eminence as "Queen of the Blues." If her father had been available, we are told, she would not be at the "Midnight Club," itself the emblem of her low social status. The name of the club suggests a critical point for the singer, the end of her day (cf. "Hattie Scott"). The title "Queen" provides the supreme irony: trapped in dissatis-factions, the Queen is powerless to command respect on her own ter-rain. Ambivalence toward men, beginning with her father and rein-forced in her relationship with "daddy," catches her between longing for love and esteem, and anger with those who withhold it.

Images are distinct and simple; color, extreme: black, brown, white, primary. The Club, in "red / With blues," suggests basic feel-ings; the "brown-skin chicken" other woman will be made "Black and blue" by the Queen. The singer's imaginary child is a "Baby girl / With velvet / Pop-open eyes," textured after her own flamboyant style.

Linguistic ironies abound. The word "holler," for example, which appears differently in the first sonnet of "Gay Chaps at the Bar," refers to the M.C. who shouts the identity of the singer as "Queen." The "holler" is an animated religious song associated with revival meetings. "Hollering" about the singer, the M.C. peddles her status like a surrogate slave auctioneer and doubly barbs the conception. Exploited by business and society, which is represented by the M.C., at the mercy of arm-pinching patrons, her position matches that of the woman who scrubs kitchen floors and is manipulated by her boyfriend, the abused woman whose life she sings, and lives.

—D. H. Melhem, "A Street in Bronzeville." *Gwendolyn Brooks: Poetry and the Heroic Voice*, (Lexington, Kentucky: The University Press of Kentucky, 1987): pp. 37-39.

EMMA WATERS DAWSON ON BLACK WOMEN IN BROOKS'S POETRY

[Emma Waters Dawson is an English professor at Florida A & M University. In this selection, Dawson analyzes the manner in which the portrayal of black women changes in Brooks' poetry.]

Prior to 1967, the dark-skinned Black woman in Brooks's poetry is intimidated by skin color and the American concept of beauty. This particular characterization is present throughout Brooks's first four volumes, *A Street in Bronzeville* (1945); Pulitzer Prize winning *Annie Allen* (1949); *The Bean Eaters* (1960); and *Selected Poems* (1963), and suggests Brooks's personal quest. However, the rejected Black woman image is relatively absent from the volumes following the 1967 "awakening," indicating the poet's affirmation of self. Relative to the presence of a personal perspective and motivation is a consideration of five important points: (1) the image of the dark-skinned Black woman's physical beauty as inferior; (2) the artistic purpose of the poet's use of this image as symbol; (3) the evidence of Brooks's projection of a personal quest through the symbol; (4) the poet's rejection of this image as symbol; and (5) affirmation of the individual through Brooks's repudiation of the symbol. The situation of the rejected dark-skinned Black woman is, accordingly, a microcosm of a larger context. The macrocosm becomes not only the limited Afro-American community, but also society in its perpetuation of color prejudice and its rejection of the individual for any reason. Gwendolyn Brooks, thus, artfully utilizes the Black woman as symbol to reflect a personal quest for self-affirmation.

To consider the first point, the existence of the image of the dark-skinned Black woman's beauty as inferior, we turn to her first published volume of poetry, *A Street in Bronzeville*. The life of women, particularly Black women, and the life of Blacks, particularly those who have grown up in the Northern big cities since World War I, figure predominantly in all of Brooks's poetry, but its presence is striking in this volume for the poet's projection of the dark-skinned Black woman as symbol. In "The Ballad of Chocolate Mabbie," there is a relative absence of time and place, indicating the poet's depiction of, perhaps, several archetypal patterns. The archetypal patterns of maturation of the young and the restriction of personal freedom become vivid through the image of the dark-skinned Black woman at childhood, a time of alleged freedom and happiness. An illustration of rejection in this poem implies no restriction of time and place; the Black woman may be intimidated at any time or any place, or as the character of Mabbie illustrates, at any age. Initially, seven-year-old Mabbie "cut from a chocolate bar/ . . . thought life was Heaven." Brooks's depiction of the theme of intimidation by skin color/beauty hints at a future of rejections. Mabbie waits "without the grammar school gates" for a little boy on whom she has a crush, but she experiences the hurt Willie Boone inflicts at his preference for the "lemon-hued lynx / With sand-waves loving her brow." Mabbie blames herself for the rejection as Brooks's use of incremental repetition exemplifies. In the six-stanza poem, the persona repeats with some variation the lines, "It was Mabbie without the grammar school gates." Stanzas 1 and 3 are identical; however, stanza 6 emphasizes, "It was Mabbie alone..." In this refrain, the words change slightly with each recurrence, sharply accentuating the ultimate isolation the dark-skinned rejected girl-child Mabbie experiences. The feeling of isolation, despite the presence of others, hints at future rejections that the child, symbolizing the rejected Black woman, will suffer. Although the point of view is that of an omniscient persona, the speaker closely identifies with Mabbie in her projection of the alleged inferiority of the dark-skinned Black woman.

—Emma Waters Dawson, "Vanishing Point: The Rejected Black Woman in the Poetry of Gwendolyn Brooks." *Obsidian II: Black Literature in Review* 4, 1 (1989): pp. 2-3.

GEORGE E. KENT ON THE REALISM OF THE POEM

[George E. Kent was a professor at the University of Chicago. He is most notably known for his work with Gwendolyn Brooks, having written two essays "The Poetry of Gwendolyn Brooks Part I and Part II." He also wrote *Blackness and the Adventure of Western Culture.* In this selection, Kent briefly discusses some themes in the poem and how they relate to Brooks' life.]

A further reach into technique and ballad form went into the elaborate work that brought forth "Queen of the Blues," a poem reminiscent of Langston Hughes's work with blues forms, but more sentimental. She wrote both poetic and prose versions of "Queen of the Blues" which show that Gwendolyn regarded the subject as a fallen woman who wished to recover her respectability. The prose version reveals the plot of a short story in the first sentence: "Ma'am Smith lounged against her work table in the ladies' dressing room of the Midnight Club, smoking while she waited for her cue, wondering if she would ever be able to get out of the mess and regain her self-respect." At 220 pounds, Ma'am Smith goes through the indignities of the nightclub scene, where she sings suggestively and the men slap her flesh and pinch her thighs. Hence "queen" is only an ironic title. As she leaves the nightclub she knocks down one man who assumes that the familiarities afforded by the entertainer are available outside the nightclub. At one point in the poetic version, she is resolved to quit her job, but the realistic ending is that she simply falls into bed in her little room. The poetic version thus has the more realistic ending but not the degree of realistic detail to be found in the prose.

"Queen of the Blues" recalled to Gwendolyn what she had seen of Chicago vaudeville and other shows on the South Side. In the blues, language is reshaped to express tough fiber, wit, contradictions of the self, salty humor, and often rituals of self-transcendence. Though overly sentimental in her concept of a downtrodden woman, Gwendolyn gets in the directness, pain, and something of the blues wit ("Found him a brown-skin chicken / What's gonna be / Black and blue") as well as a sense of blues rhythm.

—George E. Kent, "Struggles and Triumphs." *A Life of Gwendolyn Brooks*. (Lexington, Kentucky: The University Press of Kentucky, 1990): pp. 60-61.

B. J. BOLDEN ON MAME'S COURAGE

[In this excerpt Bolden discusses how the woman, Mame, in the poem is a positive figure because she is a survivor.]

. . . Mame in "Queen Of The Blues" is a survivor, but unlike Sadie, Mame is not having a good time; by contrast, her role is to provide a good time for others. The play on "the queen of the blues" recalls the history of and poetic tributes to early blues stars like Bessie Smith, "Ma" Rainey, and Billie Holiday, whose own struggles to survive were second to the balm their blues songs provided for others. Poets often pay tribute to the trials of blues queens in poems like Robert Hayden's "Homage to the Empress of the Blues" and Sterling Brown's "Ma Rainey."

"Queen Of The Blues," like "the soft man" and "of De Witt Williams on his way to Lincoln Cemetery," targets the show places and clubs in Bronzeville where folks can go to relieve the pain of their weary lives; yet only in the opening stanza is there a hint, though short-lived, of revelry for the queen:

> Mame was singing
> At the Midnight Club.
> And the place was red
> With blues.
> She could shake her body
> Across the floor.
> For what did she have
> To lose? (56)

The meager expectation for the queen to have a good time is offset by the sparse lines of the ballad and its terse language. The symbolism of vibrant red as lively abandon is cut to the quick by the resounding smack of the next line, which abruptly focuses on the "blues." For Mame not only sings the blues, she has the blues. The remainder of the ballad variation recounts not her blues songs, but her blues filled life: her "mama" is dead, she has no "Legal pa," no "Big brother," "small brother," "Baby girl" or "Sonny boy" to make her feel the shame of her profession. Her sole blues lament, accented with blues repetition, is that she cannot find "a man / What will love me / Till I die." The queen alludes to the sore consequences of her romantic alliances when she substitutes a sugar "daddy" for real parental authority. The "daddy" she was good to and loved "Found him a brown-skin chicken," after she "gave him all of [her] dough" that she earned by scrubbing floors in "white folks' Kitchens."

The only recognition and accolade the queen gets is from the emcee, and even he limits the bounds of her "Queen" stature to that of a blues star by introducing her as "Queen of the blues! / Strictly, strictly, / The queen of the blues!" The irony of her title is evident in her final query:

Men are low down
Dirty and mean,
Why don't they tip
Their hats to a queen? (59)

Brooks' women, like the "Queen of the Blues" are alive and vibrant as they struggle against the racism, sexism, classism that invade their lives.

—B. J. Bolden, "A Street in Bronzeville (1945): A Blueprint of America's Urban Landscape." In Urban Rage in Bronzeville: *Social Commentary in the Poetry of Gwendolyn Brooks*, 1945-1960, (Chicago: Third World Press, 1999): pp. 25-26.

BILL V. MULLEN ON THE STRENGTH OF MAME IN THE POEM

[Bill V. Mullen is an associate professor of Black Studies and English as Youngstown State University. He is the editor of *Revolutionary Tales: Short Stories by African American Women* and co-editor of *Radical Revisions: Rereading 1930's Culture.* In this selection, Mullen describes how through all of her problems she respects herself.]

"Queen of the Blues" on its surface most immediately recalls Sterling Brown's epic 1930s verse "Ma Rainey," Brown's most popular and arguably successful articulation of his own aesthetic program. Brown's poem famously configures the classic blues singer as an avatar of his own "Black Belt Thesis" for the emancipatory and unifying power of the rural folk tradition. Much in sympathy with Richard Wright's articulations on rural blues as the foundation of a counterhegemonic black cultural politics, Brown used "call-and-response" between singer and audience in the poem to render the transformative potential of performance for rural peasants and northern migrants. Brooks's "Queen of the Blues" bluntly engenders those themes to demonstrate their inadequacy as a liberatory model for working-class black women. Shorn of the reconstructive theoretical context of Marxian Third Period influence or a fetishized black blues aesthetic, Brooks's poem is a poetic case study resisting idealization or "meta" critical awareness for reader, author, or subject.

"Mame," the poem's protagonist, has ironically just buried her own mother and is devoid of either a socially constructed or natural family. She lacks "Legal pa," "Big Brother," "small brother," "baby girl," or "baby boy," any of whom might supply a moral or communal framework in which to evaluate her isolation. Put another way, Mame is without "front," naked, stripped down, pure product as suggested by the rhetorical emptiness and immediacy of Brooks's opening stanza:

> Mame was singing
> At the Midnight Club.
> And the place was red
> With blues.
> She could shake her body
> Across the floor.
> For what did she have
> To lose?

The poem's answer is nothing, since Mame has already lost all attachment to "decency": there are no "sweet / Sonny boy lies" to distract her from the existential or material base of her life. This deracinated conception of the blues is arguably a challenge to earlier Left and black male configurations, Brown and Wright included. Mame's laments are specific to a black female urban migrant experience as yet irreclaimable within traditional narratives of blues/folk aesthetic circa 1944 or 1945. Her request for a man "What will love me / Till I die" is rebuked by the recognition that "Ain't a true man left / In Chi;" love once given is returned only as caste insult to the dark-complected singer, like Brooks's "chocolate Mabbie," one of a number of black women stung by color and caste-conscious suitors:

> I loved my daddy.
> But what did my daddy
> Do?
> Found him a brown-skin chicken
> What's gonna be
> Black and blue.

This cycle of abusive race and gender norms is grounded in the gendered domestic economy of Bronzeville's working female poor:

I was good to my daddy.
Gave him all my dough.
I say, I was good to my daddy.
I gave him all of my dough.
Scrubbed hard in them white folks'
Kitchens
Till my knees was rusty
And so'.

As she does throughout the collection, Brooks creates metaphors of "use" and "exchange" to characterize social class formation and gendered identity. Mame's "giving away" of her domestic worker's income to an unreliable man both prefigures and is consummated in her giving away of the story of that loss to a largely male audience. Indeed, Brooks stresses the utter distance and detachment of the crowd to Mame's plaintive plea. The stanza after her lyrics are completed reports, "The M.C. hollered, /'Queen of the blues! / Folks, this is strictly / The queen of the blues!'" The dissociative indifference of the promoter to the product is mimed in Brooks's next lines, given by the speaker, whose reiteration of the opening question now carries the aftertaste of Mame's revealed pain and isolation:

She snapped her fingers.
She rolled her hips.
What did she have
To lose?

Brooks's concluding stanzas leave the bare ethnographic fact of Mame's existence as a problem in need of a solution the poem can't give:

But a thought ran through her
Like a fire.
"Men don't tip their
Hats to me.
They pinch my arms
And they slap my thighs.
But when has a man
Tipped his hat to me?"

Queen of the blues!
Queen of the blues!
Strictly, strictly,
The queen of the blues!

Men are low down
Dirty and mean.
Why don't they tip
Their hats to a queen?

In contrast to the organic consciousness and unifying voice of Hattie Jones, Brooks's "Queen of the Blues" deploys ironic slippage of voice and persona to foreground Mame's insults and injuries. Mame's fleeting "consciousness" of these injuries is interrupted by the intrusive but dislocated echo of the M.C. (now without quotation marks) as if to represent the drowning communal voice of a devouring crowd for whom her exterior performance is all. The breakdown of "call-and-response," real blues community, is implied by the disembodied reiteration of Mame's concerns in the last stanza. The problems and questions—"Why don't they tip / Their hats to a queen?—" are literally and figuratively rhetorical: call-and-response's *rhetorical inverse*. Neither Mame, the crowd, the M.C., the narrator of the poem, the authorial "persona," nor the reader of the poem can authoritatively lay claim to or responsibility for posing, or answering, Mame's lament.

—Bill V. Mullen, "Engendering the Cultural Front: Gwendolyn Brooks, Black Women, and Class Struggle in Poetry." *Popular Fronts: Chicago and African-American Cultural Politics*, 1935-46 (Urbana: University of Illinois Press, 1999): pp. 170-172.

Works by

GWENDOLYN BROOKS

A Street in Bronzeville (1945)

Annie Allen (1949)

Maud Martha (1953) A Novel

Bronzeville Boys and Girls (1956)

The Bean Eaters (1961)

Selected Poems (1963)

We Real Cool (1966)

The Wall (1967)

In the Mecca (1968)

Riot (1969)

Family Pictures (1970)

Aloneness (1971)

Black Steel: Joe Frazier and Muhammad Ali (1971)

Black Position, No. 1 (1971)

The World of Gwendolyn Brooks (1971)

A Broadside Treasury (1971)

Jump Bad : A New Chicago Anthology. (1971)

"In Montgomery" (1971)

The Black Position, No. 2 (1972)

Report from Part One (1972)

The Tiger Who Wore White Gloves or What You Really Are,
   You Really Are (1974)

Beckonings (1975)

Capsule Course in Black Poetry Writing (1975)

Young Poet's Primer (1980)

Primer for Blacks (1980)

To Disembark (1981)

Black Love (1982)

Mayor Harold Washington and Chicago, the I Will City (1983)

Very Young Poets (1983)

The Near Johannesburg Boy and Other Poems (1986)

Gottschalk and the Grand Tarantelle (1988)

Primer for Blacks (1991)

Winnie (1991)

Blacks (1991)

Children Coming Home (1991)

Selected Poems (1995)

Report from Part Two (1996)

In Birmingham (2001)

Works about

GWENDOLYN BROOKS

Baker, Houston A. Jr. "The Achievement of Gwendolyn Brooks." *College Language Association* 16 (1972): pp. 23-31.

Bell, Bernard W. "New Black Poetry: A Double-Edged Sword." *CLA Journal* 15, no. 1 (1971): pp. 37-43.

Bolden, B. J. *Urban Rage in Bronzeville: Social Commentary in the Poetry of Gwendolyn Brooks, 1945-1960*, (Chicago: Third World Press, 1999).

Brown, Patricia L., Don L. Lee, and Francis Ward, eds. "To Gwen, with Love." Chicago, Johnson, 1971. *Colorado Review* n. s. 19, no. 1 (1989).

Callahan, John F. "'Essentially an Essential African': Gwendolyn Brooks and the Awakening to Audience." *North Dakota Quarterly* 55, no. 4 (1987): pp. 59-73.

Clark, Norris B. "Gwendolyn Brooks and the Black Aesthetic" *A Life Distilled: Gwendolyn Brooks, Her Poetry and Fiction.* Eds. Maria K Mootry and Gary Smith (Urbana, IL: University of Illinois Press, 1987): pp. 90-92.

Davis, Arthur P. "The Black-and-Tan Motif in the Poetry of Gwendolyn Brooks." *CLA Journal* 6, no. 2 (1962): pp. 90-97.

———. *From the Dark Tower: Afro-American Writers 1900-1960.* Washington, D.C.: Howard University Press, 1974.

———. "Gwendolyn Brooks: Poet of the Unheroic." *College Language Association Journal* 7 (1963): pp. 114-125.

Dawson, Emma W. "Vanishing Point: The Rejected Black Woman in the Poetry of Gwendolyn Brooks." *Obsidian II* 4, no. 1 (1989): pp. 1-11.

Flynn, Richard. "'The Kindergarten of Consciousness': Gwendolyn Brooks and the Social Construction of Childhood" *African American Review* 34, no. 3 (2000): pp. 483-499.

Fleissner, Robert F. "'Real Cool' Fire and Ice: Brooks and Frost." *Robert Frost Review* (1994): pp. 58-62.

Furman, Marva R. "Gwendolyn Brooks: The 'Unconditioned' Poet." *College Language Association Journal* 17 (1973): pp. 1-10.

Gayle, Addison, Jr. "Gwendolyn Brooks: Poet of the Whirlwind." *Black Women Writers (1950-1980): A Critical Evaluation.* Ed. Mari Evans. Garden City, NY : Anchor Doubleday, 1984. pp. 79-87.

Gery, John. "Subversive Parody in the Early Poems of Gwendolyn Brooks." *South Central Review: The Journal of the South Central Modern Language Association* 16, no. 1 (1999): pp. 44-56.

Giles, Ron. "Brooks's 'A Song in the Front Yard.'" *Explicator* 57, no. 3 (1999): pp. 196-171.

Gilbert, Sandra M and Susan Gubar eds. *Shakespeare's Sisters: Feminist Essays on Women Poets,* (Indianapolis: Indiana University Press, 1979).

Guy-Sheftall, Beverly. "The Women of Bronzeville." *A Life Distilled: Gwendolyn Brooks, Her Poetry and Fiction.* Eds. Maria K Mootry and Gary Smith (Urbana, IL: University of Illinois Press, 1987): pp. 156-157.

Hansell, William H. "Essences, Unifyings, and Black militancy: Major Themes in Gwendolyn Brooks's *Family Pictures* and *Beckonings.*" *Black American Literature Forum* 11 (1977): pp. 63-66.

———. "The Poet-Militant and Foreshadowings of a Black Mystique: Poems in the Second Period of Gwendolyn Brooks." *Concerning Poetry* 10. (1977): pp. 37-45.

———. "The Role of Violence in Recent Poems of Gwendolyn Brooks." *Studies in Black Literature* 5 (1974): pp.21-27.

———. "The Uncommon Commonplace in the Early Poems of Gwendolyn Brooks." *College Language Association Journal* 30, no. 3 (1987): pp. 261-77.

Harris, Victoria F. "The Voice of Gwendolyn Brooks." *Interpretations: Studies in Language and Literature* 11 (1979): pp. 56-66.

Horvath, Brooke K. "The Satisfactions of What's Difficult in Gwendolyn Brook's Poetry." *American Literature* 62 No. 4 (Dec 1990): pp. 606-16.

Hudson, Clenora F. "Racial Themes in the Poetry of Gwendolyn Brooks." *CLA Journal* 17 (1973): pp. 16-20.

Hughes, Gertrude R. "Making It Really New: Hilda Doolittle, Gwendolyn Brooks, and the Feminist Potential of Modern Poetry." *American Quarterly* 42 no. 3 (1990): pp. 375-401.

James, Charles L. "Gwendolyn Brooks: Overview." *Contemporary Poets* 6th Ed. Ed. Thomas Riggs (New York: St. James Press, 1996): pp.

Jimoh, A. Yemisi. "Double Consciousness, Modernism and Womanist Themes in Gwendolyn Brooks's 'The Anniad.'" *MELUS* 23 no. 3 (1998): pp. 167-87.

Juhasz, Suzanne. " A Sweet Inspiration . . . of My People": The Poetry of Gwendolyn Brooks and Nikki Giovanni." *Naked and Fiery Forms: Modern American Poetry by Women, A New Tradition.* (New York: Harper and Row 1976): pp. 144-75.

Kent, George E. *A Life of Gwendolyn Brooks*. Lexington: University Press of Kentucky, 1990.

———. "Gwendolyn Brooks's Poetic Realism: A Developmental Survey in Black Women Writers (1950-80)." ed. Mori Evans (Garden City, NY: Anchor Press, 1984): pp. 88-105.

Kufrin, Joan. "Gwendolyn Brooks." *Uncommon Women*. Piscataway, NJ: New Century Publishers, 1981. pp. 35-51.

Lindberg, Kathryne V. "Whose Canon? Gwendolyn Brooks: Founder at the Center of the 'Margins.'" *Gendered Modernisms: American Women Poets and Their Readers.* Eds. Margaret Dickle and Thomas Travisano. (Philadelphia: U of Pennsylvania Press, 1996): pp. 283-311.

Loff, Jon N. "Gwendolyn Brooks: A Bibliography." *College Language Association Journal* 17 (1973): pp. 21-32.

Lowney, John. "'A material collapse that is construction': History and Counter-Memory in Gwendolyn Brooks's *In the Mecca*." *MELUS* 23, no. 3 (1998): pp. 3-21.

Madhubuti, Haki R., ed. *Say That the River Turns: The Impact of Gwendolyn Brooks*. Chicago: Third World Press, 1987.

Mahoney, Heidi L. "Selected Checklist of Material by and about Gwendolyn Brooks." *Negro American Literature Forum* 8 (1974): pp. 210-211.

Melhem, D. H. *Gwendolyn Brooks: Poetry and the Heroic Voice.* Lexington: UP of Kentucky, 1987.

———. "Gwendolyn Brooks: Humanism and Heroism." *Heroism in the New Black Poetry: Interviews and Interviews*, 11-38. Lexington: UP of Kentucky, 1990.

Miller, R. Baxter. *Langston Hughes and Gwendolyn Brooks: A Reference Guide.* Boston: G. K. Hall, 1978.

———. "'Define . . . the Whirlwind': Gwendolyn Brooks' Epic Sign for a Generation." *Black American Poets between Worlds, 1940-1960.* Ed. R. Baxter Miller. (Knoxville : U of Tennessee Press, 1986): pp. 160-73.

Mootry, Maria K. "'Chocolate Mabbie' and 'Pearl May Lee': Gwendolyn Brooks and the Ballad Tradition." *College Language Association Journal* 30, no. 3 (1987): pp. 278-93.

———. "'Tell It Slant': Disguise and Discovery as Revisionist Poetic Discourse in *The Bean Eaters.*" *A Life Distilled: Gwendolyn Brooks, Her Poetry and Fiction.* Eds. Maria K Mootry and Gary Smith (Urbana, IL: University of Illinois Press, 1987): pp. 177- 193.

Mootry, Maria K., and Gary Smith. *A Life Distilled: Gwendolyn Brooks, Her Poetry and Fiction.* Urbana: University Press of Illinois, 1987.

Mullen, Bill V. "Engendering the Cultural Front: Gwendolyn Brooks, Black Women, and Class Struggle in Poetry." *Popular Fronts: Chicago and African-American Cultural Politics, 1935-46* (Urbana: University of Illinois Press, 1999): pp. 170-172.

Owens, Clarke W. "Brooks's 'First Fight, Then Fiddle.'" *Explicator* 52, no. 4 (1994): pp. 240-242.

Pearse, Toks. "On Gwendolyn's Poem, 'The Mother.'" *Say That the River Turns: The Impact of Gwendolyn Brooks,* ed. Haki R. Madhubuti (Chicago: Third World Press, 1987): pp. 76-78.

Randall, Dudley. "Black Emotion and Experience: The Literature of Understanding." *American Libraries* 4, no. 2 (1973): pp. 86-90.

Rich, Mort. "Complexity in Plain Language: 'The Bean Eaters', by Gwendolyn Brooks," *Poetry for Students*, Gale, 1997.

Shands, Annette O. "Gwendolyn Brooks as Novelist." *Black World* 22, no. 8 (1973): pp. 22-30.

Shaw, Harry B. *Gwendolyn Brooks*. (Boston: Twayne, 1980).

———. "Perceptions of Men in the Early Works of Gwendolyn Brooks." *Black American Poets between Worlds, 1940-1960*. Ed. R. Baxter Miller. (Knoxville : U of Tennessee P, 1986): pp. 136-59.

Sims, Barbara B. "Brooks's 'We Real Cool.'" *The Explicator* 34, no. 7 (1976): pp. 58.

Smith, Gary. "Brooks's 'We Real Cool.'" *The Explicator* 43, no. 2 (1985): pp. 49-50.

———. "Gwendolyn Brooks' Children of the Poor: Metaphysical Poetry and the Inconditions of Love." *Obsidian II* 1, no. 1 (1986): pp. 39-51.

Spillers, Hortense J. "Gwendolyn the Terrible: Proposition on Eleven Poems." In *Shakespeare's Sisters: Feminist Essays on Women Poets,* Eds. Sandra M. Gilbert and Susan Gubar (Indianapolis: Indiana University Press, 1979): pp. 233-244.

———. "'An Order of Constancy': Noted on Brooks and the Feminine." *The Centennial Review* 29, no. 2 (1985): pp. 223-248.

Stanford, Ann F. "Dialectics of Desire: War and Resistive Voice in Gwendolyn Brook's 'Negro Hero' and 'Gay Chaps at the Bar.'" *African-American Review* 26, no. 2 (1992): pp. 197-211.

———. "'Like Narrow Banners for Some Gathering War': Readers, Aesthetics, and Gwendolyn Brooks's 'The Sundays of Satin Legs Smith.'" *College Literature* 17, No. 2-3 (1990): pp. 162-182.

Stern, Frederick C. " The 'Populist' Politics of Gwendolyn Brooks's Poetry" *MidAmerica* 22 (1985): pp. 111-119.

Sullivan, James D. *On the Walls and in the Streets: American Poetry Broadsides from the 1960's,* (Urbana: University of Illinois Press, 1997).

Tate, Claudia. "Gwendolyn Brooks." *Black Women Writers at Work.* Eds. Claudia Tate and Tillie Olsen. NY: Continuum, 1983.

Taylor, Henry. "Gwendolyn Brooks: An Essential Sanity." *Kenyon Review* 13.4 (Fall 1991): pp. 115-31.

Washington, Mary H. "'Taming All That Anger Down': Rage and Silence in Gwendolyn Brooks' *Maud Martha*." *Massachusetts Review* 24, no. 2 (1983): 453-66.

Wheeler, Jill C. *Gwendolyn Brooks: Tribute to the Young at Heart.*: Abdo & Daughters

Williams, Gladys Margaret. "Gwendolyn Brooks's Way with the Sonnet." *CLA Journal* 26, no. 2 (1982): pp. 215- 240.

Wright, Stephen Caldwell. *The Chicago Collective: Poems for and Inspired by Gwendolyn Brooks*. Sanford, Florida: Christopher-Burghardt, 1990.

――――. *On Gwendolyn Brooks: Reliant Contemplation*. Ann Arbor, Michigan: University of Michigan Press, 1996.

ACKNOWLEDGEMENTS

"The Woman of Bronzeville" by Beverly Guy Sheftall © 1987 from *A Life Distilled: Gwendolyn Brooks, Her Poetry and Fiction*, Eds. Maria K Mootry and Gary Smith by University of Illinois Press. Reprinted by Permission.

"A Street in Bronzeville" by D. H. Melhem from *Gwendolyn Brooks: Poetry and the Heroic Voice* © 1987 by the University Press of Kentucky. Reprinted by Permission.

"On Gwendolyn's Poem, 'The Mother' by Toks Pearce from *Say That the River Turns: The Impact of Gwendolyn Brooks* © 1987 by Third World Press. Reprinted by Permission.

From Kathryn V. Lindberg, "Whose Cannon? Gwendolyn Brooks: Founder at the Center of the "Margins'" pages 289-290, 299-301 in *Gendered Modernisms* edited by Margaret Dickie and Thomas Travisano. Copyright © 1996 University of Pennsylvania Press. Reprinted with Permission.

"Racial Themes in the Poetry of Gwendolyn Brooks" by Clenora F. Hudson from *CLA Journal 17* © 1972 by CLA Journal. Reprinted with permission from the College Language Association.

"The Bean Eaters" by D.H. Melhem from *Gwendolyn Brooks: Poetry and the Heroic Voice* © 1987 by The University Press of Kentucky. Reprinted by Permission.

"'Tell It Slant': Disguise and Discovery as Revisionist Poetic Discourse in *The Bean Eaters*" by Mary K. Mootry from *A Life Distilled: Gwendolyn Brooks, Her Poetry and Fiction* © 1987 by the Board of Trustees of the University of Illinois. Used with permission of the University of Illinois Press.

"Complexity in Plain Language: 'The Bean Eaters', by Gwendolyn Brooks" by Mort Rich from *Poetry for Students* © 1997 by Gale Group. Reprinted by Permission.

"Brooks's 'We Real Cool' by Barbara B. Sims from *The Explicator* Vol. 34, No. 7 © 1976 by Heldref Publications. Reprinted by Permission.

INDEX OF

Themes and Ideas